A Teacher's Daily Dose of Optimism

Your EQ Prescription for Thriving

Aline Kaprive

Editors: Anabel Jensen, Ph.D., Marsha Rideout

First Published in 2013 by CreateSpace

Copyright © Aline Kaprive

All rights reserved. No part of this publication may be reproduced or distributed in any form or by any means, electronic or mechanical, or stored in a database or retrieval system, without prior written permission from the publisher.

The information contained in this book is intended to be education and not for diagnosis, prescription, or treatment of any health disorder whatsoever. The author and publisher disclaim any responsibility or liability resulting from actions advocated or discussed in this book.

ISBN-13: 978-1484817483
ISBN-10: 1484817486

Design/Layout: Alison Golden
Cover Design: Caleb Jensen
Editors: Anabel Jensen, Ph.D., Marsha Rideout

For more information about bulk purchases, please contact Aline Kaprive at alkaprive@gmail.com.

Printed in the United States

This book is dedicated to the three dearest women I know: my grandmother, Helen Starkman, my mother, Muriel Johnson, and my daughter, Carly Kaprive. Together we represent four generations of amazing women who have made the world a brighter place. Thanks to each of you for being the sunlight in my life.

Grandmother: Thank you for being an inspiration and joy. I will love you forever. You are the kindest, gentlest, and sweetest lady in the world.

Mom: Thank you for being a terrific mother who taught me so much. You have a heart of gold and I love you.

Carly: Thank you for being absolutely amazing. I admire your strength, intelligence, beauty, and compassion. I could not ask for a better daughter and will always love you.

You will always be my sweethearts.

Love you,
Aline

Contents

A Personal Message From The Author   i
The Teacher's Promise   iii
Introduction   v

A Daily Dose of Optimism:
Days 1 – 185   1 – 369

Acknowledgements   371
About The Author   373
About The Editors   375

A Personal Message From The Author

My name is Aline Kaprive and I am very proud to share with you that I am a special education teacher working at the Youth Services Center otherwise known as the county juvenile detention facility.

This is definitely not your average classroom setting. I instruct at-risk students with special needs such as learning disabilities, emotional traumas, and attention deficit disorders. To make the job a little more unique, many of my students have behavior problems, countless felonies and misdemeanors, and an overall aversion to school. After fifteen years, I still enjoy my job and put my heart and soul into teaching.

What helps me with my students is that I have overcome many painful obstacles and have risen out of the ashes of a broken life. Through great pain and turmoil, I have gained the grandest of gifts - resiliency, humility, unconditional love, empathy, compassion, wisdom, and emotional intelligence.

Along my rocky path, I earned three teaching credentials, a bachelor's degree, and a Masters in Education with an emphasis in curriculum and was also the recipient of the academic excellence award from Notre Dame de Namur University. This shows that no matter how tough life gets, one still can rise up and move forward.

The Teacher's Promise

If I work diligently in teaching, keep my mind open for learning, and challenge myself, I will know what it is like to be a master teacher. I will receive all of the gifts a master teacher possesses. I will obtain all of the rewards that teaching has to offer, and truly be happy with my choice of career. I will know optimism at all levels.

I will have knowledge and wisdom for any possible situation, I will know joy, and will be fulfilled on a daily basis. I will give back to my community and to the world. I will have freedom to explore new ideas, new methodologies, and will enjoy being a progressive, motivating, and creative educator.

Aline Kaprive

Introduction

Teaching the youth of today can be challenging, rewarding, stressful, and discouraging. The demands placed on today's teachers are much more varied and difficult than ever before in history. Teachers experience the daily pressures of standardized tests, English-language learners, and special-education students (just to name a few).

Society expects teachers to take the most challenging of students and help them achieve, no matter what the circumstances. On a daily basis, many educators witness violence, disruptive behavior, and hostility. Teachers are expected to work with students who come to school with tremendous needs and enormous emotional challenges.

To be the best at our jobs, we must perform daily maintenance on our personal well-being in order to best serve our students. It isn't the day-to-day load that weighs us down, it is how we carry and manage it. If our general outlook upon life and moods is not at its best, we will be less effective with our students.

This book is dedicated to the educators of the world who need encouragement. Its purpose is to help teachers keep the fire and passion for teaching alive by providing daily support and a specific actionable step for caring for one's self. We must keep the magic alive in teaching. One answer is to give support to ourselves before stepping one toe into the classroom. A happier teacher is going to be far better able to nurture, educate, and help students.

How to use this book

Start your morning off right with a Daily Dose of Optimism. There are a couple of ways to use this book.

You can work through it sequentially from front to back, enjoying each daily page in order or you can pick up the book and flip through it until you find a page that your heart is drawn to. Read the title and quote then conceptualize the optimistic topic for the day.

Take this glorious idea and expand by applying it in the classroom. Continue reading to discover how the idea has personally affected me, a fellow-teacher, and boost your day by taking a loving action.

To solidify the Daily Dose, one must practice the "6 Second Moment" and keep a daily journal. When people are focused upon powerful loving thoughts and practice implementing them into their classrooms and daily lives, the results are eternal good for our human race.

Short on time? Read the "6 Second Moment" and use this power tip during your day.

A Teacher's Daily Dose of Optimism

#1.
Congratulations!

"If you woke up today, congratulations! You have another chance!"
Anonymous

Concept for Today

Congratulations to you for deciding to become a teacher! I honor you for accomplishing your dream and providing life-changing opportunities for the children of the world. You are spectacular, fabulous, and amazing. I pass on good wishes to each person who works in the classroom. Kudos for choosing a career in which you make a difference on a daily basis. Teaching is a wonderful profession, and you should be celebrated each and every day.

In The Classroom

"Congratulations" is an energizing word that carries so much meaning. We all like to hear the well-earned words, "Wow! Great job! Congratulations on your success!" Students love to be acknowledged. Offer many types of honors and awards at graduation, and also reward kids on a weekly basis. This can be done by displaying their work, doing a star-student-of-the-week program, acknowledging effort for improving grades, and implementing a positive reward system.

On a Personal Note...

I appreciate praise for a job well done or a noble effort so I congratulate others whenever I can.

Action for the Day

- ✓ Today, send someone a congratulatory note with an appreciative explanation. Then write about the ripples from the experience. Pat yourself on the back for being a teacher and give yourself a small reward. Also, write down three ways to honor your students.

6 Seconds Moment

- ♦ Take six seconds to congratulate yourself right now for a specific accomplishment.

#2.
Solving Problems

"When solving problems, dig at the roots instead of just hacking at the leaves."
Anthony J. D'Angelo

Concept for Today

What has been your past strategy for solving personal problems? What emotions arise? When faced with a difficult problem, what actions do you take?

Before we can rationally look at our problems and find solutions, it is imperative to be at peace with ourselves. It is much easier to solve problems if we are focused, alert, and empowered. So often, we tend to let problems consume our well-being and then we may experience panic, worry, fear, and depression. As a result, our minds, bodies, and spirits can take a brutal beating.

In The Classroom

What do you do when you feel as if you have the weight of your personal world upon your shoulders? What do you do when you feel as if you have just lost your best friend? Do you crumble and let your troubles engulf you, or do you put them aside and concentrate on your students?

There have been too many days that I have gone into the classroom feeling distressed by my own personal life.

What has really helped during these situations is briefly sharing with a colleague before class, or reducing stress by walking, or making an action plan with multiple solutions. I then tell myself that I have to put it aside for the time being and get into the moment of teaching. When I put troubles aside and concentrate on being a professional and loving teacher, my mind receives a "recess" from my problems. After school, I will review my earlier ideas about ways to solve my troubles.

On a Personal Note...

I receive the greatest gift by not allowing my personal struggles to consume me and ruin my teaching.

Action for the Day

✓ Today, when tackling problems, write them down, and brainstorm possible outcomes. This will be one step forward in solving the issue. Be patient with yourself. Don't demand an immediate answer.

6 Seconds Moment

◆ Take six seconds to remind yourself that there is power in writing down problems and making a plan of action. It is better to be engaged in the solution rather than stuck in the problem.

#3.
Contributions

"Only those who have learned the power of sincere and selfless contribution experience life's deepest joy: true fulfillment."
Anthony Robbins

Concept for Today

Teachers make such wonderful contributions to the world. They give their time, love, energy, and wisdom every day. Teachers are helping to shape the future of society by cultivating the minds of young people. Remind yourself of all the wonderful assets that you provide on a daily basis and pat yourself on the back.

In The Classroom

While working with students, we need to teach them how to give back to their community. A teacher friend of mine requires her high school class to complete at least ten hours of community service as part of their semester grade. One semester I had my seventh graders prepare and fill Christmas stockings with soap, shampoo, toothbrushes, socks, and candy for a local homeless shelter. It was beneficial to the givers as well as the receivers.

On a Personal Note…

For myself, it is important to ask, "What do I contribute to my own well being?" "How do I live by example and give back to my community?"

Action for the Day

- ✓ Today, generate new ideas for making contributions to your community, to your classroom, and most importantly to yourself. How could your staff make a contribution to the community? How could your students make a contribution to the community? Do you contribute time, love, energy, and kindness to yourself and others?

6 Seconds Moment

- ◆ Take six seconds to think of something that you can contribute to yourself as well as another human being.

#4.
Special Moments

"I'd rather have one moment of wonderful than a lifetime of nothing special."
Steel Magnolias

Concept for Today

Ask yourself if you remember the special moments throughout your day. Do you have keepsakes and pictures that remind you of special events throughout your life?

In The Classroom

In the classroom, I was having a challenging day. When I ran into a friend while walking my dog, I went through my usual venting routine and told her of all the frustrating things that had happened to me. After sharing my rotten day, it dawned on me that one wonderful thing had happened. I had a student named Charlie, who not only possessed learning and behavior difficulties but, due to an abusive upbringing, had a very hard time trusting people.

On this particular day, I was bending down getting some books off my shelf, when all of a sudden I yelled, "Ouch!" I had exercised the day before and my muscles were tightening up. As I stood up, Charlie reached over and patted my shoulder and asked, "Are you okay?" I was shocked and my heart melted. This student had never shown any empathy towards any human being. As I remembered this incident, I asked myself, "Why do I tend to reflect upon the negative components of the day and forget the special moments?" Right then and there, I decided to change this negative habit.

On a Personal Note…

I have had some very special moments in my teaching career such as when the kids had a going-away party for me because I switched teaching jobs, when one of the students sent an unexpected birthday card, or when parents told me how grateful they were that I helped their child. I understand that if I search hard enough, I can find at least one special moment each day.

Action for the Day

- ✓ Today, remember and record the special moments throughout your career. Write them down and read them when you are feeling discouraged.

6 Seconds Moment

- ◆ Before bed, take six seconds to note something special that occurred during your day.

#5.
Oxygen Is To The Lungs As Books Are To My Heart

"A book is like a garden carried in the pocket."
Chinese Proverb

Concept for Today

There is something very special about books. Reading can be used as a relaxation technique, a method to access more knowledge, or an enjoyable escape. How often do you read books just for fun?

In The Classroom

In my classroom, I work with incarcerated, emotionally disturbed high-school students. Each day, I have to deal with many challenging attitudes and behaviors. Before any learning can take place positive classroom guidelines need to be established. Dealing with students who have behavior issues truly keeps me on my toes, and I understand that throughout the day there will be outbursts. Many times, I do not get through all of my lesson plans. However, I count each day a success if my students have had quality reading time. For difficult to absorb reading material, I love to incorporate fun techniques such as reciprocal teaching, story sequencing, reader's theatre, student-generated study guides, plays, and literature circles.

On a Personal Note…

For myself, one of life's pleasures is going to a bookstore. I relish looking at and buying books that will bring pleasure into my life. Often bookstores are very supportive of educators, and I may even get a discount on these treasures. I love finding books with new activities for science, math, history, and art.

Action for the Day

✓ Today, take an inventory of the types of books that you truly enjoy reading. Schedule time to treat yourself with a new book. Also remember a special time and person in your childhood with whom you shared a pleasant reading experience. Make a list of favorite books that you have enjoyed and "sell" them to your students.

6 Seconds Moment

◆ Take six seconds to ask yourself, "Do I read before bed or watch TV? Which activity is more relaxing?"

#6.
Quotation Posters

"Quotations are important because they help to define and clarify the meanings in my heart."
Aline Kaprive

Concept for Today

Do you write a daily inspirational quote on your white board each morning? A fellow teacher practiced this ritual. One day she did not post a quote and one of her students asked her where the quote was. Please keep in mind that students are reading everything that is posted on your walls and board. Do you ever see students' attention and eyes wandering around the room? Why not try a daily inspirational quote? We affect our students in many subtle ways and may never know exactly how we have touched their lives.

In The Classroom

In the classroom, my first long-term substitute assignment was teaching life skills. I decided to have students create posters with positive life quotes. I handed out a list of fifty quotes and asked students to pick twenty of their favorites to cut out, glue onto a piece of construction paper, and decorate. After the students completed their posters, I had each student read three of their favorites to the class. The students were pleased and proud when a few other students said, "I picked the same quote." This activity helped me to improve the trust in the classroom community.

On a Personal Note…

I like to take the time to create my own quote poster. What quotes are meaningful to me? What do I discover about myself by the quotes I have chosen? This activity opens the door to my own spirit and helps me to remember what I am about as a human being.

Action for the Day

- ✓ Today, print a list of quotes and highlight those that have special meaning to you. Choose a date to make your collage and share this with a beloved friend.

6 Seconds Moment

- ◆ Take six seconds to pick a fabulous quote and repeat it. Make it a mantra for today.

#7.
Combat Disease

"To keep the body in good health is a duty, otherwise we shall not be able to keep our mind strong and clear."
Buddha

Concept for Today

What do you do when you are not feeling well? Do you listen to your body and nurture it? Or do you keep going, hoping the illness will disappear? It is extremely important to combat "dis-ease" right from the start. When referring to disease, I mean any ailment that is slowing your body down. For example, sore throats, allergies, toothaches, colds, flu, or even something more serious. Pay attention and nip the problem right from the start. Stop and pay attention, and take action. We all want to be well physically, so take the steps necessary to heal yourself.

In The Classroom

In the classroom, many new teachers report that during their first year they catch every kid's cough, cold, or flu. Veteran teachers may experience catching students' bugs when they start working with a new class. It is important to take all precautions to keep your body strong. Be aware and make your physical well-being a top priority.

On a Personal Note...

Aches, pains, and sickness discourage me. When I am ill, I can easily become depressed. However, I can choose to think positive thoughts and provide my body with extra tender, loving care.

Action for the Day

- ✓ Today, begin a new priority list in which your physical health comes first. Write down the steps that you need to take to keep yourself healthy. Medical research indicates that the best antidote for illness is exercise. Are you doing this daily? What is your plan to combat illness?

6 Seconds Moment

- ♦ Take six seconds to practice frequent hand washing.

#8.
Organization

"Sometimes the greatest gain in productive energy will come from cleaning the cobwebs, dealing with old business, and clearing the decks."
David Allen

Concept for Today

Why are the people of the twenty-first century so pressed for time? Do you believe that there is enough time throughout your day to accomplish all of your tasks?

In The Classroom

In the classroom, I value our teacher work days immensely because I can accomplish so many things, such as cleaning and organizing my supply closet, purging unnecessary files, and arranging student work. I love to clean out my bookshelves and replace the reading books with new ones that will interest kids. However, frequently there is not enough time for this. Even though it is challenging, pick a Saturday or two, or an evening or two, and organize! Make this a healing experience by letting go of unnecessary stuff. No hoarding allowed. Your classroom is like your closet; if you haven't worn that outfit for the last year, you need to let it go.

On a Personal Note...

When my classroom is organized, I feel uncluttered and my mind is clear. I know what I have and where to find things. I feel even better when my closet is organized and I can find my car keys!

Action for the Day

- ✓ Today, ask yourself how you feel when your classroom is cleaned. How does your spirit feel? Make a to-do list of things that need to be organized in your classroom. Take small steps so your goal will be met. Remember, by letting go of old, obsolete items, you are creating a space for new, stimulating materials for yourself, as well as your students.

6 Seconds Moment

- ♦ Take six seconds to pick one small organizational task that needs to be accomplished, and complete it.

#9.
Classroom Makeover

"The classroom should be an entrance into the world, not an escape from it."
John Ciardi

Concept for Today

How long have you been teaching in your current classroom? Do you like the way it is arranged? How does it feel when you walk into your classroom? Do you ever rearrange the furniture? Do you have a positive bulletin board? Where do you display the students' work?

In The Classroom

My first teaching space was the kitchen on the housing unit in Juvenile Hall. My teaching and student supplies were placed on a cart and wheeled out from the broom closet each day. I did have a bulletin board, which I could utilize, but no other supplies could be left out. Even my chairs and tables needed to be put away each day. However, as a brand new teacher, I was proud of that classroom. I made it my own, and had fun decorating my bulletin board. As time progressed, I began making positive posters for the walls and hanging up student work. I did science experiments with dyed flowers, and was allowed to keep these in the window sills behind the bars. I can't tell you how much I loved that classroom, and the students began to truly enjoy being in that space.

On a Personal Note…

I recently had an "ah ha" observation. While sitting in my room correcting papers and listening to music, I observed how pleasant it felt to be in that room. I felt a deep sense of peace and liked the way the room was arranged. I remembered that students often describe my room as a "safe" place. Atmosphere definitely matters.

Action for the Day

- ✓ Today, survey your classroom. What does it need to feel warm and inviting? What does it need to feel like your own? After all, it is your second home. Pretend that you have endless resources. What would you have in your classroom? Draw a floor plan of what your ideal classroom would look like.

6 Seconds Moment

- ♦ Take six seconds to notice something fabulous about your classroom and something to change.

#10.
The Person I Would Like To Be

"Seeing yourself as you want to be is the key to personal growth."
Anonymous

Concept for Today

We are all evolving human beings with multiple gifts. This insight is a treasure we can give our students every day. We value ourselves and we value them. In each of us there is unique potential plus the ability to achieve our dreams.

In The Classroom

In my classroom, I have a poster that says, "If you believe, you can achieve." An engaging language arts lesson is to have students write an essay on the topic, "Where will you be in five years?" Have kids brainstorm. Then tell them to write down where they would be in five years if they had a $1,000,000. Have kids share their different responses. As the teacher, reinforce for students that they can achieve their heart's desire if they believe in themselves. They may be skeptical, but send the essays home and ask the parents to save the assignments for a later time. Suggest to parents that the essays be posted in their child's room.

On a Personal Note…

One Sunday morning, I woke up worrying about money. I decided to get myself out of this funk by pondering, "What kind of person would I be if I had a $1,000,000? What would my life look like?" I then made a list which included a beautiful home, no debts, service awards, and serenity in all areas of my life. I would leave my mark in society by being a fabulous teacher who profoundly influenced each student's life, as well as a loving wife and mother. I then asked, "Why can't I have these things now?" The answer is self-doubt. I can help myself by replacing uncertainty with "I can" statements.

Action for the Day

✓ Today, make a list of both the qualities and the material items that you would have if you had a $1,000,000. Put the list in your wallet and review it regularly. There is no limit to your achievements.

6 Seconds Moment

♦ Take six seconds to state that you can and will accomplish all of your dreams. Say this six times a day for one month.

#11.
Good Food

"One cannot think well, love well, sleep well, if one has not dined well."
Virginia Woolf

Concept for Today

Everyone enjoys good food. It is used in celebrations, get-togethers, family reunions, parties, and social events. Going out for a meal is a wonderful way to replenish your body's fuel and spirit. How often do you dine out? Do you ever go out to eat with co-workers? Dining out can be a wonderful, rejuvenating experience.

In The Classroom

In the classroom, one of the nicest things that ever happened to my daughter was when she won an art contest at school, and was taken out for ice-cream by her teacher. She loved it. Also, I can recall casual school raffle functions. The prizes often included having lunch with your favorite teacher. Kids love this and it establishes an opportunity for building a bonding relationship.

On a Personal Note…

For myself, healthy food is magnificent. I feel so nourished when I eat the right foods. I know that I am showing my body gratitude. I still have to watch my intake of rich, fattening food and eat sugar-loaded foods in moderation. Most importantly, I have to be careful not to stuff my feelings with comfort food, but deal with them appropriately, by journaling, talking to a friend, or exercising.

Action for the Day

- ✓ Today, plan a night to go out to dinner with friends. Write down how often you go out to dinner and list your favorite restaurants. Remember to celebrate more often in life.

6 Seconds Moment

- ◆ Take six seconds to think of someone with whom you would like to dine and write them to join you.

#12.
Seasons Of Teaching

"Live each season as it passes; breathe the air, drink the drink, taste the fruit, and resign yourself to the influences of each."
Henry David Thoreau

Concept for Today

I often think of the different seasons of a teaching career. In the beginning, we are fresh and new like the springtime. In the summer, we are sunny, fun, hot, and spicy. In the fall, we are like trees, we are able to change colors and shed our leaves to grow new and improved ones. In the winter, we are wise, dignified, and polished like ice. No matter what season of teaching I am in, I always strive to be the best. The seasons remind us to expand and adapt.

In The Classroom

In my classroom, seasons also play a large part in my teaching themes. I use seasonal themes to enhance the environment and build student engagement. It is fun to combine science and winter by learning about snow, icicles, and the winter sky. Season themes can be incorporated into every core subject. What is your favorite season? How can you incorporate this knowledge into your content area?

On a Personal Note...

For myself, my spirit is always stretching and growing. Someday I will be a seasoned teacher, but until then I will have to face multiple seasons to arrive at my destination. Right now, I am in the season of spring, moving into summer. I am beginning to sizzle and am adding warmth and sunshine to my teaching style. It is enlightening to discover what season of life I am in.

Action for the Day

- ✓ Today, discover what season you are in by writing down the four seasons and using words that describe each. For example, words for fall might be: change, transition, letting go, and the revolution of self within your mind and body. Winter might be: polished, dignified, and wise. Spring might be: light hearted, joy, peace, and growth. Summer might be: playfulness, adventurous, and outgoing. Then sit quietly and write about your current season. Ask yourself what you need to do to become a better teacher for this season. Be gentle with yourself and know that this takes time.

6 Seconds Moment

- ◆ Take six seconds to think of your favorite season. What comes to mind?

#13.
Compliments

"I can live for two months on a good compliment."
Mark Twain

Concept for Today

How does it make you feel to give a compliment? How does your spirit feel when you receive a compliment? How often do you give them? When you do, are they genuine and heartfelt? A sincere compliment can make a significant difference in someone's life.

In The Classroom

I implement a splendid activity in which students sit in a circle and individually, one by one, bombard each classmate with a verbal uplifting compliment. Students must share something positive with each person. No put-downs allowed. After this activity occurs, a sense of well-being and friendship fill the classroom.

On a Personal Note...

When someone pays me a compliment, I am always polite but never really absorb it due to my self-esteem issues. To honor myself, I truly need to accept compliments and believe them. One day at school, a student asked me if I worked at her church, because there was a lady there who looks just like me. I told her no, and jokingly said that I must have a twin.

A few days later, I saw the student again and she commented again that I looked just like the church lady. She then went on to say, "The woman is really pretty, just like you." I was absolutely taken aback and grinned from ear to ear. Throughout the day, I noticed myself standing a little taller, and a little prouder. I caught myself looking in the mirror and saying, "Hey, I am pretty!" Due to the beautiful, spontaneous words that this girl had spoken, I truly began to blossom.

Action for the Day

✓ Today, open your ears to hear a compliment. Do not brush it off. Make a list of compliments that you have received. Save this precious paper for a self-esteem boost when you are not feeling so positive. Receive your compliments and notice the effect. You deserve it. Also give compliments in your classroom when warranted. Students deserve it.

6 Seconds Moment

♦ Take six seconds to give a compliment to a deserving individual.

#14.
Anger

"Anyone can become angry - that is easy, but to be angry with the right person at the right time, and for the right purpose and in the right way - that is not within everyone's power and that is not easy."
Aristotle

Concept for Today

Anger is a mischievous, undermining, troublesome emotion that can be difficult to manage. It can come in the form of rage, resentment, indignation, fury, annoyance, and wrath. How do you handle anger? Are you ever resentful? How often do you get angry? What is your unique process for dealing with anger?

In The Classroom

In the classroom, I not only have to manage my own anger, but deal with student anger as well. I always tell the students it is acceptable to be angry, but it is how you manage anger that counts. I help my students create plans for navigating anger. I also believe in peer conflict resolution tactics for handling those arguments over space, resources, or beliefs. Processing how to handle angry feelings can be a great journal prompt, or essay, and then, working as a whole class, students can share inventive ideas on how to manage anger.

On a Personal Note…

For myself, I need to work on anger management techniques. Many times I act first, and think later. I know that for my own well-being I do not want to go through this life angry and hostile. One technique that I discovered is going to the gym regularly to release tension. Now, I participate in a kickboxing class once a week. It is amazing how strong my punching and kicking are when I think of the issue or person that has angered me.

Action for the Day

- ✓ Today, contemplate your anger. Do you have a bad temper? Do you hold your anger inside until you explode? Is there anyone in your life who regularly pushes your buttons? Do you allow yourself to feel angry and then talk or write about it? What is your process for dealing with anger?

6 Seconds Moment

- ◆ Take six seconds when provoked to make a conscious decision to respond with calmness rather than anger.

#15.
Courage

"You gain strength, courage, and confidence by every experience in which you really stop to look fear in the face."
Eleanor Roosevelt

Concept for Today

People of the twenty-first century need courage to survive. Life can be scary, and painful. Do you face challenge with courage or flight? What is your process?

In The Classroom

In the classroom, many students have fears of which we may be unaware. There may be students who are continuously picked on, or who experience threats and bullying. As busy teachers, we may not be aware of these things. For example, my daughter's iPod was stolen from her backpack. She knew the person who had stolen it and reported him. The teacher was supportive, and they did in fact retrieve the iPod, but I wonder whether the teacher knew how worried my daughter was about this student's retaliation. As educators, we need to remind ourselves that many of our students live in fear, and teach them to communicate and search for courage. Lessons on courage can be taught in the form of mini-lessons, stories, movies, and current events that emphasize heroic acts. Discuss why the individual was able to act.

As teachers we have to remember that students may have hidden fears such as a bully, a hostile, destructive home environment, a divorce, or the loss of a loved one. Let's help our students to know true courage by brainstorming ways to cope with any and all of the above problems. Courage is taking a first step in the face of fear.

On a Personal Note...

I always tend to worry, fuss, and fret. I learned how to be courageous from my husband. My husband was diagnosed with two very frightening diseases: diabetes and hepatitis C. He never complained about his illnesses or felt sorry for himself. He would use humor in most situations. On the other hand, I was living in fear. My process for dealing with scary situations is denial. My husband, through his example, taught me to stand on my own two feet and be courageous in life no matter what. By practicing courage, I am able to grow and become empowered.

Action for the Day

- ✓ Today, practice being courageous. What steps do you need to take? Help students to find their courage as well. Plan a lesson for your students on true courage.

6 Seconds Moment

- ♦ Take six seconds to read a quote on courage.

#16.
Nurturing Yourself

"Learn the skills needed to nurture you. Ask yourself: "How do I nurture others?" and apply that to yourself."
Luke De Sadeleer

Concept for Today

Teachers are in a caregiving profession. They give and give and give. Their thoughts are on students and their unique needs, day after day. As caregivers, they need to nurture themselves before nurturing anyone else. I always think of the flight attendant's instructions before take off. "In case of emergency, put your oxygen mask on first, before putting one on your child." Practice this sound advice in all areas of your life.

In The Classroom

If you are not at your best, with your basic needs met, you will be doing a disservice to your students. Take as much time as needed to love yourself. For example, I plan my weekly lessons on Sunday mornings. Before engaging in this task, I enjoy my coffee and breakfast. Do little things to care for yourself and watch the difference in your life. Remember, once you enter the classroom, the children are your top priority.

On a Personal Note…

I behave kindly towards myself by listening to inspirational, uplifting music, exercising, sleeping an extra hour, reading a fabulous book, having a nutritious meal, getting a massage, or enjoying an intriguing movie. Most importantly, when I come home, I leave my work at the front door. Your home is for you and does not need to be invaded with thoughts of students, stresses, deadlines, planning, difficult colleagues, or troubles from school. Check your work at the front door and pick it up in the morning.

Action for the Day

- ✓ Today, focus on nurturing your spirit. When you are cared for and supported, you are a better teacher. Practice leaving your job and all of its baggage at the front door in the evening.

6 Seconds Moment

- ◆ Take six seconds for a deep, relaxing breath before you enter your home.

#17.
Optimism

"No pessimist ever discovered the secrets of the stars, or sailed to an uncharted land, or opened a new heaven to the human spirit."
Helen Keller

Concept for Today

What does optimism mean to you? When I view the world as a positive place and feel optimistic about my own life, I am a happier person. However, living with optimism is always a work in progress.

In The Classroom

Always remember that teaching is the greatest act of optimism. How can you help yourself to demonstrate optimism each and every day? How can you teach your kids to be optimistic?

On a Personal Note...

During my college days, there were many times when I felt exhausted, burned-out, and negative. Teaching school during the day and attending night classes was a challenge. I had to keep myself up and optimistic in the classroom. A technique which was quite helpful was having something to look forward to, whether it was a weekend when I could sleep in, a shortened school day, a fabulous movie on TV, or a play date with friends. It helped when I concentrated on being one day closer to graduation or a mini-vacation. I had to persevere, so being optimistic and affirming that I was moving forward was very helpful. Being optimistic means that I realize that "dark periods" are temporary, do not flood my entire life, and that I have the power to make changes.

Action for the Day

- ✓ Today, be optimistic for each moment by having a pleasant experience to look forward to, remembering a happy time, or making a difference with one of your students. Look in the mirror and affirm that you are an optimistic person and your future is bright.

6 Seconds Moment

- ♦ Before bed, take six seconds to recall something optimistic about your day.

#18.
Planning

"If you don't know where you are going, you'll end up someplace else."
Yogi Berra

Concept for Today

"I have no idea why I am teaching!" It had definitely been one of those weeks. Lessons had failed, students were not being responsible, and growth had not been achieved. It might be a good idea to take a few deep breaths, count to ten, or practice a "six second pause." In this instance, that would be to think of six reasons why you decided to become a teacher. Let the feelings of being frustrated, burned out, and incapable go. Do not carry this negative baggage any longer. When you feel like you do not know what you are doing, try one of the following: take a minute for yourself to find some peace and calmness; or try talking to another teacher in order to ask for some advice; or write down why you are feeling this way; or ask what advice your favorite author/hero might suggest.

In The Classroom

Where lessons and plans may not always work, make sure that you have a plan "B". This might include a few "Do Now" activities such as playing a game of "Mad Libs", "Eye Spy", or asking students to share the unique story behind their names. I know that for my own personal sanity, I must have back-up plans. I may be a little different from people who thrive on spontaneity, but I know that things will be more peaceful if I have an extra plan or two.

On a Personal Note...

In order to be inspired, I collaborate with another teacher and share my frustrations. When I am feeling calm, I will search for teaching lessons and strategies on the internet, read a biography on a Teacher of the Year, or go online to TeacherTube and watch a professional development teaching practices video.

Action for the Day

- ✓ Today, plan a date to make an "emergency lesson filler" file. In this file put copies of engaging books and worksheets that can be quickly integrated into your day.

6 Seconds Moment

- ◆ Take six seconds to remind yourself how calm you feel when your day is structured and planned.

#19.
Remember

"You never know when you're making a memory."
Rickie Lee Jones

Concept for Today

I was on a continuous downhill roll of having unproductive days at work. The kids were off the wall, my lessons had bombed, the principal gave me a slap on the wrist, I was exhausted and fighting a cold, my patience was limited, and each day seemed to become more difficult. March always seemed to be a time of survival, just holding on until spring break.

At home, I still had the roles of mother and wife, so at 8:45 pm, feeling miserable and exhausted, I went to run errands. I pulled up to the gas station feeling tired and stuck. As I got out of the car to pump gas, I heard my name being called by one of my former students. He was so happy to see me that he gave me a great big hug. He told me how well he was doing, and that he was finishing his diploma. He asserted that he was making better choices in life. He told me that I was the best teacher he had ever had. My heart sang and my soul surged as I thought, "This is why I became a teacher!" I was beaming with joy because I had truly helped one of my students. As I drove home, I felt a deep sense of purpose.

In The Classroom

How many former students do you remember? Do you ever see them? Do you understand the positive impact that you've had on many of your students' lives? Are you a teacher that students will remember? Think of past students and experience what emotions arise.

On a Personal Note...

I like to take time to remember the special people who have come into my life. I save pictures, letters, and old personal phone books filled with friends' numbers. I am very grateful to still be in touch with my best friend from childhood, even though she has moved away. Are there any special friends from the past with whom you remain in contact?

Action for the Day

- ✓ Today, remember a time when you made a positive, life-changing difference in a student's life. Remember that your purpose is to help students become the best that they can be.

6 Seconds Moment

- ◆ Take six seconds to remember a special student whose life you impacted.

#20.
Gratitude

"Thankfulness is the beginning of gratitude. Gratitude is the completion of thankfulness. Thankfulness may consist merely of words. Gratitude is shown in acts."
Henri Frederic Amiel

Concept for Today

Many days throughout my teaching career, I worried constantly about my lessons, supervisors, observations, co-workers, students, plus how successful each day was going to be. Perhaps a major issue had occurred at work and I believed that I had not made the best decision. To quiet my worried mind and put an end to the negative thinking, I told myself that I would practice gratitude. I made a list of things that I was grateful for, especially the little things, such as having a fluffy towel to dry off after a shower, a snack, a car that did not need repairs, or a joke my husband had told me. When I got depressed, I would pull out and read my gratitude list, written when my spirits were up. I would read the list over and over again. To be on the safe side I still carry the gratitude list in my wallet.

In The Classroom

Before I walk in, I think of how grateful I am to have a job. I then think of how grateful I am for having students who need someone to care for them. The more gratitude that I express, the more I allow positive things to flow my way. I like to teach gratitude and thankfulness lessons often, not just around Thanksgiving time. This can be done by reading stories, having students make their own gratitude lists, making gratitude calendars, or comparing their lives to someone whose challenges they do not want to have (i.e., abuse, illness, poverty, disability, etc.).

On a Personal Note…

Once when I received a pink slip and yet was fortunate enough to keep my job for the following year, I was filled with gratitude. I frequently remember this event and always give thanks for my job.

Action for the Day

✓ Today, practice being grateful for the things in your life you take for granted: your bed, home, clothes, and food. Before you enter your classroom, stop at the door, and state how grateful you are to be there with your students.

6 Seconds Moment

◆ Take six seconds to stop what you are doing, look around the room, and find two things for which you are grateful.

#21.
Laughter

"At the height of laughter, the universe is flung into a kaleidoscope of new possibilities."
Jean Houston

Concept for Today

As adults, how much do we laugh? Certainly not enough! We can learn from our students, even the noisy ones who seem to get the giggles during class. Laughter is a key to joy.

In The Classroom

Throughout our teaching careers, there will be tension and stressful situations. Negativity may occur among colleagues. For example, I had an experience one year where a great deal of pessimism and resentment filled the room as my special education coworkers met to plan the upcoming in-service. They were aware that the regular education teachers did not want to attend a full-day in-service focused on special education issues. Colleagues felt divided. Anyone who entered this room could cut the tension with a knife.

People were silent. One brave person suggested having a few general education teachers participate in the planning. The staff agreed and suggested a few teachers who would be able to help. I then asked the group, "Well, what does Debbie do?" (She was a general education teacher). The psychologist turned to the group and said, "Debbie does Dallas!" Everyone burst into uncontrollable laughter. The tension dissolved. We remembered that the purpose of an in-service is to educate all staff members, and to make it enjoyable.

On a Personal Note...

I remember to laugh. When things get entirely too serious, I think of something funny.

Action for the Day

- ✓ Today, incorporate laughter into your classroom daily routine. Write a joke on the white board and start the day by asking your students to share their favorite jokes. Show a funny video clip and have students write about it or create their own. Join in when there is a giggle in the classroom. Search the internet and find six silly jokes. Plan on sharing a joke with your students and ask them to share a joke with you.

6 Seconds Moment

- ◆ Take six seconds to think of a funny movie. Make plans to watch it.

#22.
Don't "Should" On Yourself

"Is it possible that all the horrible things you've done have been forgotten by everyone - except yourself?"
Anonymous

Concept for Today

I know I should clean the oven, should read some teacher guides, should tidy the house, should do the grocery shopping, and should go to the bank. I should wash the car and vacuum. I should lose weight. Oh no, I should have done that in class, I should have finished that project yesterday, should have called that parent and should have spoken with the principal. I definitely should have taken an inventory of my school supplies.

When you "should" on yourself, you are really putting yourself down. Instead, boost your self-esteem by making a list, and if you accomplish a task, praise yourself. If you do not accomplish any of the tasks, recommit for tomorrow. Perhaps you have said something that you regret. Forgive yourself. Decide that you will not repeat the error in the future.

In The Classroom

As a student, I can recall being told I should have done this, or I should have done an assignment a certain way. Teachers made me feel discouraged. Many times I would get the correct answer in math, but did not solve the problem the way the teacher wanted me to. This used to upset me terribly and I grew up hating math. Think before you "should" on your students.

On a Personal Note...

I still tend to put myself down when I make a mistake, rather than perceive the situation as a learning opportunity. I am slowly learning not to "should" on myself. Remember the saying, "E is for effort." I believe that if I have tried my best, then all is well. I do know that there is always room for improvement, but I try to commend myself for trying my best.

Action for the Day

- ✓ Today, think about whether you ever put a guilt trip on yourself or "should" on yourself. Are you critical or loving towards yourself? Which attitude will bring you comfort when you make a mistake? Write your thoughts on guilt trips and "should-do's". Erase the word "should" from your vocabulary.

6 Seconds Moment

- ◆ Take six seconds to forgive yourself when you make an error. Open your mind and see what you can learn from the situation.

#23.
Abundance

"When you are grateful, fear disappears and abundance appears."
Anthony Robbins

Concept for Today

Sometimes in life, we may feel that we are lacking in material things. We may think that we do not have enough money, time, or items that bring us joy. We may feel that we do not have enough teaching materials to support our lessons. Now is the time to open ourselves to the abundance of life. Life provides us what we need and desire if we turn our energy around and focus on abundance rather than scarcity.

I woke up this morning telling myself, over and over, that I have abundance in every part of my life. I stopped and paid attention to how this positive statement affected my moods and realized that it changed my perspective. This is not a selfish or silly act. Thinking positively, saying the words, "I have abundance in all areas of my life," allows good things to flow toward me.

In The Classroom

In the classroom, we were planning projects for Mother's Day. We needed thirty small jewel-size boxes that I could not find. A friend went to an art store and found little boxes for $3.00 a piece. This was, in my opinion, too much money. (It is amazing to me how much money teachers spend out of their own pockets). The next day, I kept thinking, "I have abundance in all areas of my life." After school, I went to the mall (still thinking positively) and went to the gift wrap counter. I told the man that I was a teacher and about our need. He was so kind, and donated thirty beautiful boxes for our Mother's Day project. This is a small example of how abundance can work in our lives.

On a Personal Note...

I must remember to repeat positive words to myself and then, most importantly, allow myself to have things. Instead of thinking "I can't," I think "I can and will!"

Action for the Day

- ✓ Today, allow abundance into your life because you deserve it. Make a list of things that you want in life, big or small, and focus on the possibility of acceptance. Allow positive energy to pour into every aspect of your life. We can never have too much love, connection, joy, or happiness. As human beings, it is also okay to have the little and big things in life that bring us ultimate joy.

6 Seconds Moment

- ♦ Take six seconds to say, "I am abundant in all areas of my life." Repeat this throughout your day.

#24.
Sparkle And Sparklers

"A smile is a curve that sets everything straight."
Phyllis Diller

Concept for Today

Do you consider yourself a vibrant and enthusiastic person? Does your personality sparkle? Do you live your life to the fullest? Do you have charisma? Are you lively? Are you fun to be with? Do you consider yourself outgoing and adventurous? If not, what can you do to add a little sparkle to your personality?

In The Classroom

When I plan my daily lessons, I create all of them with the goal that each will shine and appeal to all learners, but one lesson will stand out and really sparkle. I call these lessons my sparklers. A sparkler is a lesson that will be both entertaining and interesting for all students. A sparkler lesson may be a hands-on project, an enjoyable video, a multi-media presentation, an art project, reading a play out loud, listening to a song and analyzing lyrics, having kids come to the board to demonstrate a concept, or working in small groups. Since I teach multiple subjects, incorporating a daily sparkler lesson is a bit easier. If I were teaching a single subject course, I would plan for one part of the lesson to be particularly intriguing and engaging. To maintain my energy level, I incorporate a balance between high-intensity teacher support, and low-intensity teacher support for all lessons. As far as my needs are concerned, I know that I am caring for myself by balancing teacher-led activities with student-led activities.

On a Personal Note…

I am married to a man who should have had a career as a stand-up comedian. Next to him, I was serious, dull, dry, and boring. That is until I became much more confident as a teacher. To my surprise, I developed a sense of humor and a more sparkly personality. This effervescent personality arose and a joyful self-assurance blossomed. My husband still wins the award for best comic, but I strengthen my sparkly personality each and every day.

Action for the Day

- ✓ Today, be a teacher who sparkles. To do this, try to make sure that you are feeling good mentally and physically. Make sure your teeth are sparkly, your attitude sparkles, and that your eyes sparkle when you communicate with others. Write down a plan for where your lessons may sparkle or when you will let your personality sparkle.

6 Seconds Moment

- ◆ Take six seconds to uncover the sparkle in your personality.

#25.
No Put Downs

"Laughing at our mistakes can lengthen our own life. Laughing at someone else's can shorten it."
Cullen Hightower

Concept for Today

It is neither fun nor productive to put one's self down. We need to be kind to ourselves when we make mistakes. We need to forgive ourselves immediately and move forward.

I can remember being a teacher's aide for a nursery school. One of my duties was to clean the restrooms. I worked hard and had done a spectacular job cleaning toilets, sinks, and the mirrors. My last task was to mop the floor. I filled the bucket with soap and water and was getting ready to mop. I then accidentally tripped over the bucket and spilled the soapy water all over the floor. I had a major flood. Right at that moment, my boss walked in. I was embarrassed and ready for a reprimand. I was criticizing myself for being stupid when she smiled at me and said, "That floor is going to be so clean." I relaxed and cleaned up the mess. Putting myself down was not necessary.

In The Classroom

In my classroom, I collaborate with students to create class rules. I listen to students and take their suggestions, but still manage to get the very important rule of "No Put Downs," added to the list.

On a Personal Note…

I have to practice the art of "No Put Downs" for myself before I can instill this rule in my classroom.

Action for the Day

- ✓ Today, if you are self-critical, stop immediately. When teaching, if you hear a student "put down" another student, deal with the situation calmly and quickly. Have a mini-conference with that student in a kind but firm manner and place your positive attention on the student who was "put down," by giving him/her mini-praises and kindness.

6 Seconds Moment

- ◆ Take six seconds to catch self-criticism and say, "Cancel, cancel, cancel."

#26.
A Taste Of Stone Soup – Interdependence

"There is no delight in owning anything unshared."
Lucius Annaeus Seneca

Concept for Today

Have you ever heard of the story entitled, "Stone Soup: An Old Tale" written by Marsha Brown? It is a whimsical tale about how a hungry man pretends to make the most delicious soup with stones. He draws in the attention of the town's people who previously had not helped this poor, starving man. They are intrigued with the man's soup. Eventually, they borrow food from their own cupboards in order to add these precious ingredients to make a truly delightful concoction, which all can share and enjoy.

There is something healing about soup. It may bring back special memories of your grandmother's kitchen, the feeling nurtured by eating soup on a cold winter's day. Where in your life have you allowed people to help you? Do you create an idea and add richness to it by using others' ideas? Do you begin with one idea and accept others' input? One tradition that is absolutely beautiful is the dressing of the bride on her wedding day. To fully complete her outfit, she must borrow something special to wear. It is also reasonable to rest upon your friend's shoulders and borrow an idea.

In The Classroom

Before I read the story of "Stone Soup" and before the lesson is initiated, I ask the students to each bring in a vegetable. When everyone is gathered with vegetables in hand, I share that with only one ingredient, the soup will be insufficient, but when everyone shares their wonderful vegetables, the end result is a magnificent repast.

On a Personal Note...

I am very independent and, at times, like to work alone. This is certainly valuable, but independence should be balanced with interdependence.

Action for the Day

- ✓ Today, brainstorm a lesson plan in which students will need to share with one another.

6 Seconds Moment

- ◆ Take six seconds to appreciate the contributions of others.

#27.
Education

"An education isn't how much you have committed to memory, or even how much you know. It's being able to differentiate between what you do know and what you don't."
Anatole France

Concept for Today

We are teachers! We have a marvelous opportunity to guide and educate the generation of tomorrow. As teachers, it is very important to remember that we also are continually learning and, to be the very best at our jobs, we must remember that we are still students.

In The Classroom

In the classroom, most teachers are provided two in-services per year. This is not enough. To be the best at our jobs, we need to stay updated with new trends in teaching. How do we do this in our busy lives? Taking a few minutes to read a teacher's guide, searching the internet for new methods and lesson plans, or perhaps participating in a seminar of personal interest. We can always practice with technology and use visitation days to observe a veteran teacher. The youth of today are sharp. I must remember that I am a teacher who doesn't simply have a job, but am improving upon "my craft." I continue to progress and educate myself weekly.

On a Personal Note...

I read the newspaper to stay up to date on current events. I also read books and watch educational television programs. Much of my learning takes place in the form of research on the internet. I know in my heart that I must never stop learning.

Action for the Day

✓ Today, take ten minutes to read a teacher's guide for a subject that you teach and highlight the key concepts. Write down two methods or ideas for improving a lesson. Think of an idea for improving your "craft." Remind yourself that you care for yourself by exercising and strengthening your brain for a few minutes each day.

6 Seconds Moment

♦ Take six seconds to tell yourself that you are educated, that your lessons can be brilliant, and that you will continue to learn.

#28.
Plant Your Feet Firmly On The Ground And Keep Your Head In The Clouds

"A grounded person is 'in the moment'–aware of their thoughts and of the people around them."
Eva Dahm

Concept for Today

As human beings, we are all aware of the energy inside ourselves and around us. Grounding means breathing in and centering ourselves. We allow our energy to run into the earth. Being well grounded helps you deal with life in a secure and rational manner. Everyone has special moments, moments when one seems to "feel grounded". When I "am grounded", I am free to make appropriate choices.

In The Classroom

In the classroom, can you recall days when you were alert, focused, and centered? How does your day play out when your feet are firmly planted (you are aware of your body and space), and your mind is open to creativity, love, and intuitiveness? How can you arrive at such a state of peacefulness? We can take steps to adopt this attitude by living in the moment, breathing deeply, and thinking positively. I love those teaching days when I am in the present moment, and centered.

On a Personal Note...

For myself, personally, I am not a master of planting my feet firmly in the ground with my mind fully open. I always need practice. Many times, I know that I am not grounded, because all of my energy is in my noisy mind. When this occurs, I realize that I need to balance my energy and free my cluttered mind.

Action for the Day

✓ Today, write down what it means to have your feet planted firmly in the ground and to have your head in the clouds. How often do you feel completely at peace and balanced? How can you bring more centeredness into your life?

6 Seconds Moment

◆ Take six seconds to stop, plant your feet in the ground, and free your mind.

#29.
Teacher Appreciation Day

"You, yourself, as much as anybody in the entire universe, deserve your love and affection."
Buddha

Concept for Today

How do you show appreciation towards others? Are you a person who is thoughtful and caring? Do you remember to send birthday cards and thank you cards? Wouldn't it be wonderful if we took time to show appreciation for ourselves?

In The Classroom

In the classroom, May 14 is the official Teacher Appreciation Day, but we can acknowledge ourselves daily with a short nap, a favorite TV program, a soothing bath, or cup of tea, exercise, or leisure reading time. Set a goal to finish school and home tasks early leaving some quality evening time for personal choices. So many times, I have forgotten to appreciate myself and have turned into a "human doing" rather than a "human being."

On a Personal Note...

For myself, the needs of others often tend to come first. It takes practice to appreciate myself daily.

Action for the Day

✓ Today, let's appreciate ourselves and continue to do so each day for one week. Write down seven ideas that will allow you to appreciate yourself each day and follow through. During the week, take mental notes to see if you are feeling better because of this self-love.

6 Seconds Moment

♦ Take six seconds to remind yourself of how you will appreciate yourself for today.

#30.
Scrub-A-Dub-Dub

"Reflect upon the defects of your character: thoroughly realize their evils and the transient pleasures they give you, and firmly will that you shall try your best not to yield to them the next time."
Helen P. Blavatsky

Concept for Today

How do you feel when you take a shower and wash away all of the grime and dirt? Usually after a shower, we feel cleansed and energized. We may feel fresh and new. Do you ever feel as if you need a shower or bath on the inside? Do you have character defects and shortcomings which should be washed away? It is fabulous to be clean on the outside, but often we need a scrub-a-dub-dub with our personality and character. Is there anything that you would like to change about yourself, such as a short temper, irritation, gossiping, or self-centeredness? Ask yourself if you feel spotless on the inside. Reflect upon your life and ask if your side of the street is clean and shiny.

In The Classroom

In the classroom, teachers will encounter students who have poor behavior or shortcomings that need to be washed away. How can we help students get rid of funky, displeasing behaviors? We can talk with students, set up behavior plans which allow for success, and utilize reward systems. Children need to be built up, rather than wounded and broken. Think of your own life, when you make a mistake at work. Would you gain more being reprimanded, and criticized, or given feedback that will improve your work performance? Let's help our students to scrub-a-dub-dub unpleasant behaviors away.

On a Personal Note...

For myself, I know that I have character flaws, and shortcomings. By acknowledging that there are parts of my character that are less than pleasing, I am able to make a change for the better. If there is a behavior that truly does not fit me anymore, I make a decision to get rid of it by writing about it, stopping myself when I am practicing it, and discussing it with a good friend. I know that I will never be perfect. I acknowledge I can change useless behaviors and dissolve my character defects.

Action for the Day

✓ Today, write down your character blemishes and cleanse with nourishing thoughts.

6 Seconds Moment

◆ Take six seconds to think of one character defect that you have and decide to change it.

#31.
Noisy Minds

"Do not anticipate trouble or worry about what may happen. Keep in the sunlight."
Benjamin Franklin

Concept for Today

Did you know that individual teachers make over six thousand decisions per day? We are always thinking, thinking, and thinking. Our decisions affect so many other people. Sometimes our minds act like radio receivers taking in not only our problems but everyone else's. I know that I am overloaded mentally when I dream about my job, or go to bed with racing thoughts about work.

In The Classroom

Recognize how cluttered and noisy students' minds can be. We cannot know everything that happens to them at home or in their lives. To help students clear their minds, have them journal as soon as they enter the classroom.

On a Personal Note…

Someone told me it is not healthy to listen to the television news before you go to sleep at night, because you may end up dreaming about the horrible things that are going on in the world. I stopped watching the news before bed, but I still had a noisy mind about students, teaching, deadlines, mistakes made, troublesome parents, kids not grasping concepts, and so forth. I hate thinking and worrying about work before going to sleep. To turn off my noisy mind, I read an inspirational book, practice thinking good thoughts, repeat a positive affirmation, or listen to a relaxation CD. I quiet my mind before bed.

Action for the Day

✓ Today, practice quieting your mind. Make a commitment to not think about work or troubles before bed. Write down one method for quieting your mind. Find an affirmation that works for you and repeat it.

6 Seconds Moment

◆ Take six seconds to rest your mind and be absolutely quiet.

#32.
Frustration

"I've come to believe that all my past failure and frustrations were actually laying the foundation for the understandings that have created the new level of living I now enjoy."
Anthony Robbins

Concept for Today

Things in my life had been building up. I was experiencing frustration with the little things in life, such as traffic, bills, my teenage daughter's attitude, a sick husband, and the tough demands at work. So many things seemed to be going wrong and I was truly frustrated. The only positive thing in my life was the fact that I could easily identify frustration.

Frustration is not a pleasant emotion and it can lead to anger. What can I do to ease my frustration? I can take a break and remove myself from the distressing situation. Since my adrenaline has increased, a brisk walk, sharing with another human being, or writing about it are helpful techniques. If I am in the car and am aggravated with traffic, I can turn the music up louder or listen to a self-help CD. I repeat to myself that this too shall pass.

In The Classroom

In the classroom, this must be how my students feel when they cannot grasp a lesson or have failed a test. One positive thing about dealing with my own frustrating situations is that I can experience first hand what my students may be feeling in the classroom. For students, I can suggest taking a little recess from the challenging task, or show them how to break down the assignment so they can succeed, or perhaps offer an alternative lesson to the current one.

On a Personal Note...

My heart screams when I am frustrated. My emotional levee is close to breaking, my fists clench, and the tears well-up. Instead of pulling my hair out, I can be pro-active and work frustration out by deep breathing, and when calm, re-examining the situation.

Action for the Day

✓ Today, ask yourself what really frustrates you. What events can you recall at work that were exasperating for you? How did you handle the situations? How do you help a frustrated student?

6 Seconds Moment

♦ Take six seconds to sit down and identify six coping mechanisms for frustration to avoid its escalation.

#33.
Here Comes The Sun!!!

"Spring is nature's way of saying, "Let's party!"
Robin Williams

Concept for Today

Each school year, I look forward to springtime. After the cold, wet weather, the dreariness, and the seasonal blues, I always feel recharged when the weather turns warm and sunny. Sometimes I count the days until spring, and even get excited when I see the pre-spring clothing commercials on TV.

In The Classroom

In the classroom, springtime warms my heart and strengthens my teaching. There are so many wonderful things to teach in the spring. Simply going outside and feeling the sun on my shoulders revitalizes me. I take this new energy into my classroom. I like planning a lesson in which students can go outside. We may do still-life drawing, a springtime art project, look for ideas from nature to inspire a poem, garden, or go on a field trip to study marine biology at the beach.

Sometimes I like to have older students study the composition of different bubble formulas and then go outside to chart which bubble solution will be the strongest. People seem to be in better moods when there is sunlight.

The happy news is that by this time in the school year, I feel that there is not only sunshine outside, but, if all has gone well, a trusting classroom community, and a positive relationship between me and the students.

On a Personal Note...

I know that I suffer from seasonal depression. To help myself, I have my rooms filled with lots of light and take Vitamin D. Bring in a plant or flowers to add life to your classroom.

Action for the Day

- ✓ Today, appreciate the sun. Let its warmth brighten your soul and your teaching. Plan an outdoor activity or a field trip for your students. Get out of your comfort zone and take your students outside to do their regular work. There is something very special about the sun. Write down how springtime and sunshine affects you personally and in the classroom.

6 Seconds Moment

- ♦ Take six seconds to stand in the sunlight, and take mental notes as to how the sun makes you feel.

#34.
Irritability

"Holding on to anger is like grasping a hot coal with the intent of throwing it at someone else; you are the one who gets burned."
Buddha

Concept for Today

Have you ever observed yourself acting cranky or irritable during your day? There are many possible reasons, such as not sleeping well, a cold, or receiving some bad news. Perhaps you have had an argument with someone you love.

In The Classroom

There have been times when I have caught myself being annoyed with students. Their outbursts and side conversations aggravate me. My patience is limited, and I speak before thinking. Unfortunately, my students know when I am feeling moody and will bluntly confront me. This embarrasses me and makes me feel unprofessional. Of course, I respond honestly, but I then immediately put myself in check and make a huge effort to be courteous. How do I do this? By thinking before I speak, practicing a "six seconds pause," or stepping back for a moment. I can manage my emotions.

On a Personal Note...

I have to think through the irritability. I need to do something to help myself move past this emotion. I do try to think of something positive in my life. Irritability also gives me a fund of information about other people. It tells me that something is wrong and instead of passing a judgment, I need to be more supportive. I also take someone else's crankiness as a sign that they may need to have some space. I used to make it my fault when someone was irritable towards me. Now I honor people and their different emotions; however, I have chosen not to be a doormat and bear the brunt of someone's bad temper.

Action for the Day

- ✓ Today, think of how often you get moody or irritable. What triggers this emotion? What is your process for dealing with irritability at home, and in the classroom? What do you do when others are irritable?

6 Seconds Moment

- ♦ Take six seconds to make a commitment to move past the emotion of exasperation. Know that it is reasonable to have any emotion, but handle it appropriately.

#35.
Everyone Hurts

"Suffering has been stronger than all other teaching, and has taught me to understand. I have been bent and broken, but I hope into a better shape."
Charles Dickens

Concept for Today

Each and every person has experienced some form of hurt. The hurtful times in life have helped us to evolve into who we are today. We have developed compassion and empathy for others. We are better teachers after going through personal trauma. Our students will never know our personal sorrows, but we have evolved into stronger, more loving human beings. Since we have experienced broken hearts, disappointment, and hurt, we can appreciate and love life more fully.

In The Classroom

In the classroom, when students experience painful situations, I am able to offer support. My high school students experience many daily hurts and to be the type of teacher who can offer a kind word, or a shoulder to cry on, makes me an empathetic educator.

On a Personal Note...

When I was going through my difficult times, I couldn't figure out why terrible things were happening to me. All I knew was that my world seemed to be ending. I now recognize that if I hadn't experienced the hurts and wounds in life, I would not appreciate the joy and happiness of my life today. I hate the hurtful times, they break my heart. However, I am able to love more deeply as a result.

Action for the Day

- ✓ Today, if you are feeling hurt, talk about it with another person. Allow yourself to feel the pain and cry if need be. Do not stuff your feelings. Know this will pass. When you are out of "hurt" mode, make a list of suggestions to use when you're experiencing darkness, such as walking the dog, helping someone else in need, or repeating "life is good."

6 Seconds Moment

- ♦ Take six seconds to give a smile to another human being. Ask how they are and listen thoughtfully to the response. They could be hurting.

#36.
Self-Talk

"You've done it before and you can do it now. See the positive possibilities. Redirect the substantial energy of your frustration and turn it into positive, effective, unstoppable determination."
Ralph Marston

Concept for Today

I woke up this morning feeling scattered, overwhelmed, and tired. It was the first morning back to work after vacation. I was experiencing the grieving process due to my holiday having ended. Yes, I was tired. Yes, I wished that I were still on vacation. Yes, I wasn't quite ready to go back to work. I looked in the mirror and told myself that I was a competent teacher, over and over again. I told myself that I would create a good day. I then went to the kitchen and washed the pile of dirty dishes. I reminded myself to get into the moment and wash the dishes with mindfulness and thoroughness. While doing so, I kept telling myself that I am a great teacher and that today would be a great day. I was replacing the negative thoughts with positive ones.

In The Classroom

In the classroom, it is important that your own self-talk be optimistic. It regulates your behavior. It is imperative that you are a confident, loving teacher. For my students, I am always trying to cement the idea into their heads that they are winners. I have frequently caught my high school students in Juvenile Hall putting themselves down! They appear so tough, but when they use negative self-talk it indicates that they are very vulnerable and do not have a lot of self-confidence.

On a Personal Note...

I need to always work on improving my self-talk. I would never talk to another human being the way I sometimes talk to myself. What this shows me is that I need to keep working on my self-confidence and self-forgiveness when I make mistakes.

Action for the Day

- ✓ Today, replace negative thoughts with positive ones. Remind yourself that today is going to be terrific. If you begin to feel negative, focus your attention on the task at hand and cancel out the negative thinking. Write down tasks that can get your mind off depressive thoughts.

6 Seconds Moment

- ◆ Take six seconds to stop outside your classroom and commit to yourself that you will not indulge in negative self-talk.

#37.
Crystal Vision

"We do not perceive things as they are; we perceive them as we are."
Anaïs Nin

Concept for Today

Many teachers are extremely intuitive. They read their students on a daily basis and tune into their unique needs. Have you ever prepared a lesson plan and rehearsed it until you knew it forward and backwards? These lessons are winners and will flow smoothly. We can visualize how our lessons will play out in the classroom. Crystal vision means seeing a lesson, implementing it, and feeling thrilled that it just went smoothly and students were engaged. Crystal vision also means being in tune with ourselves, physically, mentally, and spiritually. We know how we are feeling, are in the present moment, and feel a sense of vision and purpose in our lives. Diaphragm breathing can support crystal vision.

In The Classroom

In the classroom, have a clear vision as to how you want the environment to appear. I have a vision for my students, and hope to help them have clarity about their own life and their choices. What is your vision for your classroom and students? Do you teach students to have an optimistic vision for their futures?

On a Personal Note...

I enjoy the moments when I experience crystal vision. During these moments, I can clearly visualize my goals and objectives, and use my "mind's eye" to achieve exactly what I want for the day. To tap into my crystal vision, it is imperative that I slow down and draw on my intuition and wisdom.

Action for the Day

- ✓ Today, remember to breathe from your diaphragm and free your mind. Tap into the vision you want to have for yourself. Write about a time where your vision for a lesson flowed and worked for both you and the students.

6 Seconds Moment

- ◆ Take six seconds to observe your breathing and remind yourself that you need to inhale and exhale from the diaphragm.

#38.
Worry

"There is a great difference between worry and concern. A worried person sees a problem, and a concerned person solves a problem."
Harold Stephens

Concept for Today

Excessive worrying is a pointless exercise and cruel obsession, which can wreak havoc in our lives. Are you a worrier? If excessive, irrational worrying is a part of your core, what can you do to help yourself?

In The Classroom

In the classroom, I often think about students who worry about tests. Some students will literally make themselves sick with worrying. As a loving educator, how can I ease their worry? If I act like a coach, I can give them positive pep talks, help them to be fully prepared for the exams, and provide them with strategies for studying and test taking.

On a Personal Note...

I have always been a worrier. Perhaps I was born that way. I worry about every little thing, such as whether I left the front door unlocked, or the oven on. Have I left the coffee pot turned on? This irrational worrying has created a stressful existence for me. I learned to deal with my worry by practicing a few techniques: 1) writing down my worries; 2) distracting myself with productive tasks; 3) seeking counsel from a beloved friend who can help me to put my worry into perspective. Sometimes when faced with a crisis, I think of the worst case scenario and prepare myself for it. Interestingly enough, hindsight reveals that when it came to my worrying, the worst case scenario rarely ever occurred!

Action for the Day

✓ Today, rate yourself on how often you worry. Are your worries rational? Does worry consume a great deal of your time? How do you help yourself when you are worried?

6 Seconds Moment

♦ Take six seconds to release the worries which are harmful or out of your control.

#39. Motivation

"Shoot for the moon. Even if you miss, you'll land among the stars."
Brian Littrell

Concept for Today

How do we keep ourselves motivated, and continue to improve our teaching practices? What does it take to complete boring, routine tasks that we do not care for, or to learn new teaching techniques when we feel overwhelmed? We need motivation in our own lives and we need techniques to keep our students motivated.

In The Classroom

In the classroom, my hope would be that students are motivated by the desire to learn. Unfortunately, this is often not the case. Grades can be a strong motivator, but not always. This is why I use points and reward systems at Juvenile Hall. It amazes me how responsive students are when it comes to earning points and seeing their names written on a poster displaying how many points they have earned. The reward? They earn a wonderful letter which is sent to their probation officers. They also win caffeine-free and sugar-free flavored water. If I were teaching in a regular educational setting, students would be rewarded with healthy snacks and field trips.

On a Personal Note...

For myself, in high school and community college, I had very little motivation to succeed and had not acquired any self-discipline. One reason may have been that I had failed at so many classes that it was expected by teachers, as well as myself. As I grew older, I learned ways to motivate myself. For example, I would make a to-do list and, if tasks were completed, I would be able to watch a favorite TV show in the evening, take a nap, or have a special dinner. I also gave myself pep-talks to keep motivated. Planning was very important. If I scheduled one hour after school to grade papers, than I could be free to enjoy the rest of my day free of school-related thoughts and deadlines.

Action for the Day

- ✓ Today, step up your teaching and give yourself a positive self-talk to truly shine before the next holiday.

6 Seconds Moment

- ◆ Take six seconds to set a realistic goal, something which you have been postponing regularly. Also, think of how you will reward yourself when you achieve this goal.

#40.
Improving Our Lesson Plans

"The life of the creative man is led, directed and controlled by boredom. Avoiding boredom is one of our most important purposes."
Saul Steinberg

Concept for Today

Remember when we graduated from college and had our first teaching assignment? We were filled with hope, energy, and creativity. New teachers have so many unique ideas. As the years pass, we may get stuck in a rut with our lives and teaching. To avoid this, we need to add pizzazz both to our lives and lesson plans.

In The Classroom

In the classroom, I had a wonderful lesson which I had prepared for my first teaching assignment. I called it, "Amusement Park Physics." Each year, I enjoy teaching this unit but like to add something to it, such as a video, a virtual reality tour on a roller coaster, a kit with which students build models of amusement park rides, or even a field trip. I keep the teaching concept, but improve upon the unit each year by adding an enhanced component. This exercise only takes a few minutes and everyone benefits. I nurture myself by stretching my creativity. I feel proud when I present winning lesson plans.

On a Personal Note...

I realize that it is a gift to be able to plan lessons and make improvements. I can take the gift of planning and apply it to my own life. For example, I can plan how to manage my money and make improvements, I can plan a trip and make it really fun, or I can plan meals and spice them up. Being able to plan is a treasure that helps life run smoother.

Action for the Day

- ✓ Today, look over your lesson plans and add a new emotional component. Find a new aspect to add interest to one of your lessons. Nurture your creative mind and write down a new idea for old lesson plans which will hook students.

6 Seconds Moment

- ◆ Take six seconds to read a "creativity" quote.

#41.
Savor The Flavor

"Don't dig your grave with your own knife and fork."
English Proverb

Concept for Today

How often do we practice eating good food and taking the time to eat slowly? Do we sit down for meals anymore? What do mealtimes look like at your house? Are they rushed and frantic, or calm and rejuvenating?

In The Classroom

In my classroom, we study good nutrition. Cooking is a great way to learn math and science, as well as healthy eating habits. Incorporate some cooking lessons into your curriculum. One activity that I love is called Multi-Cultural Salad. I buy several different types of vegetables, cut them up, and place them into bags. I get a big bowl and have kids come up, introduce themselves, and their nationality. They then pour the contents of their bag into the bowl. After everyone has done this, I say that one vegetable tastes good by itself, but when all of the vegetables are mixed together, we have one wonderful super salad. Nutrition and cooking can be incorporated into any subject matter area. Kids love it.

On a Personal Note…

I tend to eat on the run. In the mornings, I am so hurried that sometimes I forget to take lunch. Luckily, I will not go hungry at work because there is usually some junk food in the teachers' staff room. I need to re-focus and eat properly. Is it possible to slow down and eat healthy food in the correct portions? It is really sad that even with a teaching credential in Health Science, with my busy career and life, I don't practice good nutrition consistently. My goal is to listen to my body and take time to shop, plan, and eat properly. I started changing my eating habits when my husband was diagnosed with Type II diabetes. We met with a nutritionist and the first task was to keep a food journal. Slowly but surely, I have incorporated some good eating habits. Good nutrition is always a work in progress.

Action for the Day

- ✓ Today, plan nutritious meals for your body. Sit down when you eat and remember to drink plenty of water throughout the day. Keep a journal regarding your own personal eating habits. No matter the age of your students, plan a nutrition or food activity in your subject area.

6 Seconds Moment

- ◆ Take six seconds to slow down and remind yourself to chew each mouthful of food in order to savor the flavor.

#42. Collaboration

"Never doubt that a small group of thoughtful, committed people can change the world. Indeed, it is the only thing that ever has."
Margaret Mead

Concept for Today

One thing that you need in your life is positive people. I love going to in-services where I am surrounded by many different educators. Collaboration is extremely important for expanding my creativity and boosting my lessons. I need to meet with co-workers not only for collaboration, but celebration as well, in recognition of growth, achievement, or accomplishment. Among colleagues we have formed a leadership committee which tackles school issues and improved practices. This is very invigorating because each person gets to choose an area of personal concern. My area of interest was finding grants. My supervisor told me that as an inclusion teacher, she had found marvelous grants. She then gave me key words to search for them. Two heads are always better than one, especially when it comes to lesson plans and school improvement issues.

In The Classroom

In the classroom, I also enjoy having students collaborate. Some of the best learning and greatest projects come from cooperative working groups.

On a Personal Note…

For myself, collaboration with my family members is extremely important. We must listen to one another in order to strengthen our relationships. This practice seems to be more challenging with family but with patience, active listening, and open communication, collaboration can be achieved.

Action for the Day

- ✓ Today, think of a special person with whom you work. Offer to collaborate on a unit. Perhaps you know someone who might like to offer support. What dream would you like to make a reality? With whom could you collaborate to achieve it?

6 Seconds Moment

- ♦ Take six seconds to choose a special person with whom you would enjoy working. Ask them for their help.

#43. Seek

"Only as high as I reach can I grow, only as far as I seek can I go, only as deep as I look can I see, only as much as I dream can I be."
Karen Ravn

Concept for Today

As educators, we need to seek new material, new ideas, new knowledge, and new trends in technology. What about our own lives? Are we seeking to better ourselves? Do we seek understanding and love? Do we seek our highest good in life? Do we seek loving friendships and trust? Do we seek adventure and optimism?

I simply existed for many years. I was on the road of survival throughout my life. In fact, I liked my comfort zone. I did not want to seek anything new or deal with change. At times, I was self-seeking. My mother told me not to be selfish, but inside I was. Through the cuts and bruises of life, I learned to seek my higher good without being stingy or self-centered. Inside of me, I desperately sought a better way which would allow me to risk and to grow.

In The Classroom

When I was in high school and community college, I hated school. I never sought knowledge and only cared about protecting myself. I did not know how to seek a better life. It was through major pain and suffering that I learned to appreciate joy and laughter. I can now take this experience and empathize with my students.

On a Personal Note...

For myself, I now seek new adventures in life for I know I will learn from them. I am continuously seeking my highest good. What are you seeking in life? Have you committed to establishing a "noble goal"?

Action for the Day

✓ Today, remember to keep your eyes and ears open. Indeed, keep your mind open and look for the possibilities in your life.

6 Seconds Moment

◆ Take six seconds to make a list of what you are seeking in your personal life.

#44.
Forenoon: Much Too Early

"When I wake up in the morning, I just can't get started until I've had that first, piping hot pot of coffee."
Emo Philips

Concept for Today

How do you face the morning? Are you a morning person? A dog may wake up gently or may wake up barking and ready to attack. Which represents you? What does your morning routine look like? Are you rushed and stressed, and do you tend to oversleep? Are you overwhelmed in the morning and feeling frantic? Perhaps many of your negative mornings are perpetuated by allowing yourself to wake up on the wrong side of the bed.

In The Classroom

In the classroom, my students often come in tired. Many times they fall asleep in class. If a student falls asleep, I gently wake him or her. If they just cannot stay awake, I tell them to go to the restroom and splash water on their faces. As a teacher, I do not know if my students have eaten breakfast, or gotten enough sleep. A fellow teacher did the following: asked her students to donate one dollar each, then went out and purchased milk, bread, peanut butter, and jelly. She assigned two students each week to be in charge of making the sandwiches. The teacher charged one dollar and twenty-five cents for a sandwich and glass of milk. She would then use the money to replenish the supplies. This morning ritual only took about ten minutes of class time and started everyone out on the right foot. If a student was hungry and had no money, she extended credit. As a result of the peanut butter and jelly ritual, her students were more awake and ready to learn.

On a Personal Note…

For myself, I just do not start functioning at my best until after 10:00 am. By understanding this about myself, I can adjust my morning routine to make it successful. I will sometimes rise a little earlier in order to enjoy my coffee and take my time entering the world. I try very hard to be gentle with myself.

Action for the Day

- ✓ Today, write down what your morning routine looks like on weekdays as well as weekends. Are you a morning person? What are your typical thoughts during the weekday mornings? What about your children?

6 Seconds Moment

- ◆ Take six seconds in the morning and say, "I love you" to everyone in your home, including yourself.

#45.
Jealousy

"The disease of jealousy is so malignant that it converts all it takes into its own nourishment."
Joseph Addison

Concept for Today

Jealousy is a valid emotion. Recognizing our motivation, then determining an appropriate response, can build character. Do you know someone who is the jealous type? Is it a positive way to spend your time?

In The Classroom

In my classroom, I am aware of my treatment of students and do not allow favoritism.

On a Personal Note…

I used to be very jealous of other people. If my husband talked to another female, I would burn inside. When the teachers received a raise but the Para-educators did not, (I was a Para at the time), I would experience deep resentment. If something wonderful happened to another person, I would be secretly envious. In my youth, I was never truly "glad" for someone else's good fortune. What a waste of time and precious energy.

Recently, I even experienced jealousy of other teachers when they did not receive a pink slip and I did. This emotion can be exhausting and produce negative outcomes. Once, I observed someone very close to me exhibit extreme jealousy. She was absolutely positive that her husband was cheating on her and, as a result, was a very unhappy woman. I sincerely wished that this woman could move past her acrimony.

By strengthening my own self-esteem, I have released the need to be jealous and can truly be glad for someone else's happiness. What a revelation to learn this life lesson! When someone tells me about a trip that they will be taking, or that something wonderful has happened to them, I am truly thrilled. Honestly being excited for another's good fortune allows positive things to come my way.

Action for the Day

- ✓ Today, spend some time on introspection and be honest with yourself regarding jealousy. If you are jealous of someone's good fortune, choose to recognize your own by writing down all of the things for which you can be grateful.

6 Seconds Moment

- ◆ Take six seconds to tell yourself harboring jealousy is not productive.

#46.
A Good Cry

"When I feel overwhelmed and my stress levels rise, I stop and step back from the situation and put the event in perspective. I always ask myself, 'What difference will this make in five years' time?'"
Catherine Pulsifer

Concept for Today

Have you ever felt as if a levee was going to break any minute? As a child, were you taught that it was wrong to cry or show emotion? What is your process for those times when you are feeling burdened and overwrought?

In The Classroom

In the classroom, teachers have so much on their plates that they may feel distraught. Things build up, and build up, until the "straw" breaks the camel's back, or in this case the teacher's spirit.

A co-worker had been administering the STAR Test to her ninth-grade students. The students were absolutely fried, misbehaving, and unruly. After administering the state tests for one week, my friend was called into the principal's office after school. The principal spoke with her about being more lenient with the stressed-out students. Even though the principal was courteous and kind about the reprimand, it still upset my friend's equilibrium. She needed a few minutes for a good cry. Afterwards, she felt a sense of relief and clarity. The next day she went into her class, saw her students with much more compassion, and was able to implement positive, effective discipline. She told me that she felt much better after her emotional release and did, in fact, appreciate the principal's advice.

On a Personal Note...

Sometimes I need an emotional outlet to release intense feelings. A good cry is extremely healing for the body. Keeping overwhelming feelings bottled up inside eats away at our souls and bodies. It could be very useful to create a lesson for students based upon "the straw that broke the camel's back." Let students brainstorm about what the straw might represent. Then they can write about a solution.

Action for the Day

- ✓ Today, write in your journal about the last time you released frustrating feelings. What did you do to help yourself when the pressure escalated?

6 Seconds Moment

- ◆ Take six seconds to be by yourself and identify strategies to manage your emotions.

#47.
On The Spot

"Leadership has been defined as the ability to hide your panic from others."
Anonymous

Concept for Today

What do you do when you are a "up a creek without a paddle?" What if someone puts you on the spot and wants an explanation or an answer that you are not comfortable sharing? Have you ever been in the hot seat, when you needed to either think quickly or make amends?

In The Classroom

Have you ever been a substitute teacher? I have and at times have felt panic, confusion, and disorder. One night while working as a substitute ESL teacher (English as a Second Language), I came into the classroom and discovered that there was no lesson plan.

Frantically, I began looking for something to improvise with. I found a book of vocabulary BINGO games and another worksheet book. Saved! (Or so I thought). Then, I discovered that the copy machine was broken. I was in a pinch. I took the two books back to the classroom and found that I had thirty adults to teach and no lesson.

I took a deep breath and pretended everything was normal. I introduced myself and asked each student to share their name and something special about themselves. Based upon this conversation, I did an informal assessment about their English abilities. I then said that we were going to play a game called "Picnic."

It went well and then I grabbed a teachable moment and discussed singular and plural nouns. On my break, I found some worksheets on this topic and found a different copy machine. By remaining calm and acting as if everything was under control, the class ran beautifully.

On a Personal Note...

I have discovered that if I am on the spot, my thinking accelerates and I am able to make decisions. If you are under pressure, are you able to think and act quickly?

Action for the Day

- ✓ Think about what you would do if you were caught without a lesson plan and appropriate materials. Which lesson and assessment would you use?

6 Seconds Moment

- ♦ Take six seconds to identify the emotions around a recent panic. Take another "6 seconds" to brainstorm some solutions.

#48.
Pink Slips And Lay-Offs

"Loss leaves us empty - but learn not to close your heart and mind in grief. Allow life to replenish you. When sorrow comes it seems impossible - but new joys wait to fill the void."
Pam Brown

Concept for Today

Losing your job, whether it is in the form of a layoff or termination, is a scary experience. A deep sense of fear may creep in, and it may even turn into panic. Our jobs mean survival for ourselves and our families.

In The Classroom

In the classroom, after three years of challenging assignments, I found myself in my dream teaching position. Everything was glorious and I was really getting into a rhythm of how teaching worked. On March 15th, I came to work like any other day. I was making copies when the principal asked to see me. I did not know that March 15th was D-Day for teachers. The principal issued me a pink slip and asked me to sign, confirming that I had received it. I almost fell off the chair. I was in major shock and felt like someone had knocked the wind out of me. To add insult to injury, when I got home, I found a letter confirming that the district would no longer need my services for the upcoming school year.

After the pain and shock subsided, I took action. Since I was in the union, a lawyer was assigned to my case. Inside I felt nothing but fear. However, by standing firm and taking the risk, my pink skip was rescinded. However, I still face transfers and pink slips each year. Would I have gone into the teaching profession if I had understood the seniority process? Absolutely! Now when I think about pink slips, I just accept them as a part of the job.

On a Personal Note...

I wish that there were no layoffs and that everyone could be employed. I like the merit system and wish that teachers were rewarded for the wonderful work that they do rather than how long they have been on the job. If unemployment comes my way, I will go through a grieving process and then persevere by looking for a job. I will never give up, because I was born to be a teacher.

Action for the Day

- ✓ Today, write about the risks of pink slips, layoffs, and transfers. Is it worth the risk to go into the teaching profession? Why or why not? What would you do in case of an unwanted vacation?

6 Seconds Moment

- ◆ Take six seconds to remind yourself to always have a "back-up plan."

#49.
Acting As If...

"Press on. Obstacles are seldom the same size tomorrow as they are today."
Robert Schuller

Concept for Today

Sometimes I experience the "grumpies". However, I cannot go to work and yell at the kids or my boss or co-workers. Keeping myself busy and acting "as if" everything is normal is a reasonable thing to do. I do not want to stuff my emotions, but I also do not want any scenes at work. I have to rise above the discord in my life and "act as if…"

Suppose a student really pushes your buttons. Suppose your car broke down on the way to work. Suppose you did your semester grades and lost the only copy. We cannot run and hide, we have to act professionally. I have been screamed at by a parent yet remained calm and collected, when I wanted to retaliate.

In The Classroom

In the classroom, I work with kids on probation who possess short fuses. In some of their classrooms of the past, these students were kicked out for losing their tempers. Instead of isolating them, we need to teach coping skills. For example, I could remind them to sip water, take a break from the group, do six jumping jacks, etc. I, also, need to model for them appropriate behaviors by sharing stories of how I learned the negative power of anger.

On a Personal Note...

I can recall my best friend from childhood telling me to "shine it on" when I was feeling less than positive at school. She taught me to practice saying "Hello" and "Good morning" to as many people as possible and to try and keep a smile on my face. This practice worked and after "shining it on" I received the gift of having people say hello to me.

Action for the Day

- ✓ Today, write down your own coping skills for when you get angry. What do you do with an angry parent? An angry co-worker? Create a lesson for your students on anger management and dealing with difficult situations.

6 Seconds Moment

- ◆ Take six seconds to practice taking slow, calming breaths.

#50.
Relax

"If a man insisted always on being serious, and never allowed himself a bit of fun and relaxation, he would go mad or become unstable without knowing it."
Herodotus

Concept for Today

Isn't it great to go on a vacation and just relax? Wouldn't it be fantastic if we could just get up and go on vacation any time that we like? Unfortunately, this is not reality. The good news is that we can take time throughout our hectic days for mini-vacations, anywhere and anytime by taking a few deep breaths. Sometimes, instead of having lunch in the noisy teachers' break room, I will go and have lunch in my car and listen to music. We can relax before bedtime by having a cup of hot tea and reading a favorite author. We can watch a sunset, talk to a friend, or take a power nap. Scheduling breaks is a necessity for long-term teacher survival.

In The Classroom

In the classroom, I have observed that if I am relaxed, my students are more apt to relax. Students feed off my moods. I like to start my teaching day by playing soft music and having kids do journaling. This activity allows students to release the stresses which they are carrying. Each student then takes a mini-vacation before the day starts.

On a Personal Note...

For myself, there was one terrible year when relaxation was just out of reach. It was the year my husband was sick. It was the year that I taught very low-functioning, middle-school autistic students, wrote my thesis, and was the mainstay for the family. As a result, I became cranky at home, developed neck and back problems, and lived in a consistent negative emotional state. I now ask myself why I never took a relaxation break. Yes, I had to meet deadlines, but a mini-vacation would probably have increased my efficiency. I cannot change that year, but I can learn from it.

Action for the Day

✓ Today, schedule time to relax. Write down three techniques for helping students relax in the classroom. Put them into practice.

6 Seconds Moment

◆ Take six seconds to find the tension spot in your body. Deliberately tighten the muscles in that area and then relax. Repeat as needed.

#51. Waterfalls

"Climb the mountains and get their good tidings. Nature's peace will flow into you as sunshine flows into trees. The winds will blow their own freshness into you, while cares will drop off like autumn leaves."
John Muir

Concept for Today

Waterfalls are gorgeous parts of nature. They are clean and clear and breathtaking. The sound of a waterfall is extremely comforting. When I am feeling frustrated, I think of a waterfall and imagine all of the anxiety rushing down and falling into puddles at my feet. I visualize love and fresh energy pouring in like a fountain refreshing my spirit.

In The Classroom

In my classroom, I have a colorful poster with a luxurious waterfall, green river, and ocean animals. It presents color, beauty, and peace in my room. It is a soothing element for both students and their teacher.

On a Personal Note...

One of the happiest times in my life was staying in Northern California in the mountains. The lady who owned the property had a waterfall and I actually took a shower in it. When I need to reconnect with "happiness" I visualize that moment.

Action for the Day

✓ Today, visualize and remember a part of nature that fills you with joy and makes your heart sing. Fill your classroom with posters showing nature at its best. What form of nature soothes your soul? Do you have an image that can bring you instant peace? Write down your favorite "image in nature" and the feelings that it evokes.

6 Seconds Moment

◆ Take six seconds to observe and appreciate two forms of nature such as a tree, flowers, or the green grass.

#52.
Playful Spirit

"If you want to be creative, stay in part a child, with the creativity and invention that characterizes children before they are deformed by adult society."
Jean Piaget

Concept for Today

I really enjoy being in the company of all children. They have such wonderful, playful spirits. Working with youngsters reminds me of my own child-like spirit. Kids teach me the value of innocence, playfulness, and joy. How do I tap into my playful spirit? I do so by acknowledging my inner child through journaling. I can remember the little person inside of me and remember to show kindness to her. When I am trying to fall asleep, I tell her that I love her. Someone once told me that we all have inner children. I thought this was silly, but came to realize that this is in fact, true. I have experienced my inner child or child-like spirit when exploring and finding my curiosity. Some examples include going to the amusement park, or to the zoo, taking a dance class, doing an art project, or listening to the music of my youth.

In The Classroom

In the classroom, when I was preparing for my first teaching assignment, I searched on the internet for ideas. I then connected the ideas with lessons and classes that I had enjoyed as a child. I was drawn to an amusement park unit. Since I had loved amusement parks so much as a child, I felt sure that my students would not only love the unit, but would learn and remember. They did.

On a Personal Note...

For myself, a special friend sent me an online Nickelodeon cartoon coloring book, from the animated show "As Told By Ginger" created by Emily Kapnell. It was a gift for my inner child. What gifts do you give to your inner child?

Action for the Day

- ✓ Today, ask yourself if you are nurturing your inner child. Is there a playful aspect to your general demeanor? What do you do to bring out your lighthearted spirit? Perhaps you dance and do the "shimmy", or ice-skate, or play loud music, or paint, or sing in the shower. My joyful spirit comes out when I am driving. I have always dreamed of being a rock star, so I do most of my rehearsing in the car. I know that I am providing the world a great service by keeping my window rolled up!

6 Seconds Moment

- ◆ Take six seconds to pick a song that you know and love and rehearse it in your car.

#53.
Deadlines

"A perfect method for adding drama to life is to wait until the deadline looms large."
Anonymous

Concept for Today

Deadlines can cause major stress and pressure. They also can be used as motivators and guidelines for meeting goals. How do you handle deadlines? Are they a positive or negative experience? Deadlines can make us frantic and give us hurry sickness. Many people wait till the last minute before completing a task or project and seem to thrive under pressure. I do not flourish under pressure. When I wait to the last minute, I feel nothing but worry, tension, and anxiety. I would rather use deadlines to help me rationally plan and organize.

In The Classroom

In all classrooms, students have deadlines. As teachers, how do we help students to manage their time and meet deadlines? I provide them with a sample timeline on how to break down reports and projects into manageable steps. I also provide calendars with due dates and five check-off sections, which help students divide the assignments into measurable chunks.

On a Personal Note...

For myself, there was a time when I would wait until the last minute to get things done. There is nothing in the world less enjoyable than doing your income taxes on April 15th, two hours before midnight. Sometimes I would miss my deadlines and then I would be filled with guilt and looking for excuses. I discovered it to be more efficient (and less anxiety producing) to set specific goals with measurable objectives and coordinating due dates.

Action for the Day

- ✓ Today, write down your process for meeting deadlines. List any changes that you would like to make. If you perform better under pressure, be grateful for this gift.

6 Seconds Moment

- ♦ Take six seconds to decide the benefits of being a planner and another "6 seconds" to identify the costs of being a procrastinator.

#54.
The Ambience Of Hogwarts School

"We can choose to function at a lower level of awareness and simply exist, caring for our possessions, eating, drinking, sleeping and managing in the world as pawns of the elements, or we can soar to new and higher levels of awareness allowing ourselves to transcend our environment and literally create a world of our own – a world of real magic."
Wayne W. Dyer

Concept for Today

All classrooms need magic. It could be in the form of a delightful math problem, a creative writing assignment, an enchanting play or a fantasy reading assignment. Or the magic could occur when an emotional hook is used that engages learners. For younger students, consider the introduction of the legends of Ireland, such as the Leprechauns during the month of March or making razzle dazzle masks and costumes which celebrate Mardi Gras. My own classroom becomes delightful when students feel at ease, safe, and intrigued about learning. By enriching my lessons and adding a dynamic touch to them, enchantment comes to my class. I recommend: enchantedlearning.com. While the site is written for younger students (ages 3 to 10), the ideas can be adapted for older learners.

In The Classroom

In the classroom, I recall times where the magic of Harry Potter and the Hogwarts School, developed by J. K.

Rowling, created an impetus for learning for very difficult students. One student hated to write but insisted on presenting an oral book report on "The Sorcerer's Stone". I presented to him certain situations that Harry might face and got the student thinking and writing critically. By adding a little pizzazz to my teaching approach, this student developed and strengthened his writing practice.

On a Personal Note...

For myself, I must keep life magical. By exploring new ventures, taking risks, and watching the magic when a student grasps a concept for the first time, I can keep the enchantment alive.

Action for the Day

- ✓ Today, pretend that you are a professor at Hogwarts School. What will your lessons look like? How will you teach good versus evil? What will your philosophy be? Have fun and write down your ideas. Note the magic that occurs in your classroom.

6 Seconds Moment

- ◆ Take six seconds to think about the magic in your life.

#55.
Philosophy

"Life is a pure flame, and we live by an invisible sun within us."
Sir Thomas Brown

Concept for Today

Are you a philosopher? Do you consider yourself a wise person? Do you ponder the meaning of life? Do you consider why there is so much pain and suffering? Do you stop and think about the stars and universe? What about life after death? Are you a deep thinker, or so rushed that you forget to consider such abstract thoughts? Stretching our brains and reflecting on such issues can create more meaning for our daily life. We also need a philosophy for teaching.

In The Classroom

In the classroom, what is the educational philosophy for your school? Is it posted in your classroom? Do you recall writing your teaching philosophy when you were in the credential program? From time to time, it is a good idea to review and add to your list. It would be beneficial to post your teaching beliefs somewhere for students to view. It is very valuable to construct your teaching viewpoint, and even more important to consider your personal value system and teaching beliefs intertwined.

On a Personal Note…

To remember who I am and what I stand for, I like to write down my philosophy. I ask myself questions such as, "What are my positive characteristics? Am I a role model? Do I help others? Am I unique? Do I lie or steal? Am I lazy? What gifts do I offer other people? What do I like about myself? Do I possess honor and valor? Am I a carefree spirit? Do I enjoy life? What are my morals? Do I do unto others what I would like to have done to me?"

Action for the Day

✓ Today, write down three quotations to consider for your personal philosophy. Plan for some free time to brainstorm possibilities and begin to develop your life philosophy.

6 Seconds Moment

◆ Take six seconds to pick a date to write your personal life philosophy.

#56.
Toes And Feet

"I cried because I had no shoes, then I met a man who had no feet."
Anonymous

Concept for Today

How often do we pay attention to our feet and toes? Perhaps it is only for thirty seconds in the shower. I am a teacher who is constantly on my feet. I walk around monitoring students, I stand in front of the class, I hurry to get somewhere, but I often forget about the value of my feet. I may pay attention for a minute if my feet hurt. How often do you pay attention to your feet? Our feet and toes are important and we need to care for them.

In The Classroom

In my classroom, I have an insightful shoe activity for learning math and measurement. Students will take off one shoe and use it to measure the perimeter and area of the classroom. This activity can also be used for measuring the playground, gym, or basketball court. Students can measure their desks with their shoes. To enhance this activity, provide an explanation of how feet and yard measurement came to be.

On a Personal Note...

For myself, one day I took a yoga class and one of the first exercises was to put my feet on the mat and stretch each toe and then flex and point my foot. To my surprise, there was an ugly corn on my big toe. How was it possible that I had not noticed this? How long had it been there? I had been so busy that I had not noticed that my feet were uncomfortable.

Action for the Day

- ✓ Today, pay attention to your feet and toes. This will put a smile on your face. Write down your plan for caring for your feet and toes.

6 Seconds Moment

- ♦ Take six seconds to get off of your feet.

#57.
Self-Expression

"Everybody who is human has something to express. Try not expressing yourself for twenty-four hours and see what happens. You will nearly burst. You will want to write a long letter or draw a picture or sing, or make a dress or a garden."
Brenda Ueland

Concept for Today

Remember when you were in high school and self-expression was a top priority in your life? How did you dress? Were you casual, nerdy, artsy, or preppy? Did you have cool posters on your walls and purple hair? As an adult, we still need to exhibit self-expression on a daily basis.

In The Classroom

In the classroom, encourage students to express themselves. I help students to know that they are valued and appreciated as unique individuals. I witness their self-expression through art, work, journals, hair color, and music preferences. My goal as teacher is to let students know that they are valued, as they are. I guide them to express themselves academically, artistically, and individually. My hope is that students never lose their sense of spirit and unique qualities, and that individuality is not to be forgotten. Allow your students to let their inner differences shine.

On a Personal Note…

For myself, I ask the question, "How do I express my uniqueness in the classroom?" One way is the music which I play during quiet times, work times, or discussion times. Secondly, I have an "I Love Lucy" poster hanging in my classroom. Two ways of self-expression are not enough! I need to open my mind and discover additional likes and interests. One fine way to express myself is having clothes that are "me." I do not need to dress as "frump" girl anymore, and can start wearing clothes that shout out my individual personality. I know if I take the time, I can figure out other ways of self-expression. A wonderful friend of mine expresses herself by wearing unique jewelry and clothes that are in the Middle Eastern tradition. She has a style that is all her own.

Action for the Day

- ✓ Today, be open to demonstrating self-expression. Write down ways that you can show the world your individuality.

6 Seconds Moment

- ◆ Take six seconds to notice one way that you reveal your self-expression in your home, classroom, and clothing.

#58.
Aesthetics

"For every beauty there is an eye somewhere to see it. For every truth there is an ear somewhere to hear it. For every love there is a heart somewhere to receive it."
Ivan Panin

Concept for Today

In your life, what awakens and delights your senses? Does your school décor nurture and inspire you? Where are the aesthetics in your classroom? What about your desk? Is this pleasing to your senses? How does your classroom smell?

Teachers are creative people who need inspiration on a daily basis. We need to bring our senses alive in our day-to-day routine. We can do this by adding color, flowers, fun pillows, beautiful pictures, candles, and art work.

In The Classroom

In the classroom, I cannot be productive unless the room has space, light, and pleasing colored pictures. I like to present a welcoming environment in which kids can learn. Since I spend so much time in my classroom, I need to be pleased with my environment.

On a Personal Note…

When I feel upset or anxious, I like to practice looking around and finding one thing that pleases my senses. For example, if I am waiting in line at the bank, I look for one piece of beauty. It might be another human being, the way that the light shines through the windows, or something unusual on someone's desk.

Recently, I had an eye-opening experience. It was a lovely, spring day, and I woke up feeling positive and serene. As I drove to work and entered the parking lot, I observed how lovely the sunshine was as it shimmered down upon the school building. I took a moment to view my surroundings and gave a silent word of thanks for my school and my teaching job. I set the foundation for a pleasant day and carried this appreciation into my classroom.

Action for the Day

- ✓ Today, write down five things that are aesthetically pleasing in your classroom and make a list of additions needed to help awaken the senses of your students. Purchase one small item at a time.

6 Seconds Moment

- ♦ Take six seconds to observe your surroundings and find one thing that is pleasing to the senses.

#59.
Helping Another

"She said it grieves me so to see you in such pain, I wish there was something I could do to make you smile again."
Paul Simon

Concept for Today

Research indicates that an effective way to get out of a bad mood, depression, or self-pity is to help another human being. Do you reach out to others? Between a one and a ten (one being the least), where do you rank yourself as a friend?

My heart breaks when I see loved ones, friends, and anyone else in emotional pain. I wish that there was something I could do to relieve their suffering. My heart breaks even more when my students are hurting.

In The Classroom

In the classroom, I work with high school students who not only have special needs, but have had traumatic things happen to them during their lives. When I hear their stories, I just want to cry. I know that besides being a good listener, I can help my students even more by providing the best instruction possible and teaching them that there is an alternative to their previous choices. I teach my students to empower themselves and, at the same time, to be empathetic and to help others.

On a Personal Note...

For myself, I have often gone to bat for my friends and co-workers in order to help them in any way possible. I model for my students the significance of being a valued friend. I lend support when teachers confront adversities. They have shared how much it means that I truly care.

Action for the Day

✓ Today, lend a hand to another human being. Evaluate and rate yourself as a friend. Remember that if life depresses you, the best antidote is service to others.

6 Seconds Moment

♦ Take six seconds to ask someone how they are doing and really listen to their response.

#60.
Denial

"The worst lies are the lies we tell ourselves. We live in denial of what we do, even what we think. We do this because we're afraid."
Richard Bach

Concept for Today

When we experience hurt or troubles, we might tend to deny it. Denial seems to ease our pain, but only temporarily. We work hard to stuff pain deep down inside of us. The hurt may have occurred during childhood; however we still carry it, and deny that it is there. To be the best that we can be, we have to move away from denial. Admitting there is hurt or a problem is half way to being healed. How many times per week, when asked how you are, do you reply "Fine?" I often tell myself that I am being courteous, and this may be appropriate in the circumstances. But are we really fine, or are we trained to suppress our real feelings? When dealing with denial it is important to acknowledge the situation, become honest, journal about it, or talk to a trusted friend.

In The Classroom

In my classroom, I deal with denial quite often. My students carry the weight of the world upon their shoulders and have seen so much sadness in their short lives. However, when asked about it, they shut down. Please don't let this happen to your students. I work very hard to build a trusting environment and special rapport with my kids, so that, if in fact something is bothering them, they can come to me.

On a Personal Note...

For myself, denial has caused emotional damage. By pretending that a situation is not real, I cheat myself. The truth may hurt, but there will be no painful secrets or dishonesty. As a child I was taught never to tell a lie, however, I did not understand that this also meant I should not lie to myself. We cheat ourselves when we engage in denial.

Action for the Day

- ✓ Today, write down the areas in which you are in denial. Make a plan to acknowledge your feelings and move forward. To be the best teacher that you can be, you must first remove your own personal darkness, so you can shine light on others.

6 Seconds Moment

- ◆ Take six seconds to ask yourself if you are in denial about anything, big or small.

#61.
Getaway

"Vacation used to be a luxury, however, in today's world, it has become a necessity."
Anonymous

Concept for Today

Just like children, teachers need recesses and breaks from school. To rejuvenate our spirits and honor ourselves, we can plan a wonderful weekend away. The benefits are plenty. We can laugh, discover something new, visit friends or relatives, and embrace our inner child. By having a fabulous getaway planned, our moods are uplifted, we have inner anticipation and excitement, and our attitude towards work becomes more positive.

In The Classroom

In the classroom, when I know that I have plans to get away, something special happens to my disposition. I think to myself, only so many days until my trip; therefore, I am going to be the best teacher possible until then. I will provide intriguing and fascinating lessons. Since I have something so wonderful to look forward to, I will shine during my week before the trip. Also, by determining that I will have a wonderful week at school before embarking on a trip, I am able to allow myself to have a long, well-deserved recess. Getaways are like water to the dehydrated traveler lost in the desert.

On a Personal Note…

For myself, it is imperative that I have getaways. A co-worker, who has been a master teacher for over twenty years, explained to me that she needs her time away. If she doesn't take time, she will become exhausted, worn-out, and then will be shark meat in front of her students. Students can "smell" when you are vulnerable.

Action for the Day

- ✓ Today, look at your calendar and plan a special getaway. Know that the holiday can happen at anytime, and by having a fabulous weekend trip planned, you are lifting your spirits and filling yourself with anticipation. Get out your calendar and plan a trip. Write down when it will be, and where you will go. Write down how you will feel.

6 Seconds Moment

- ♦ Take six seconds to pick the month that you will be going on your next getaway.

#62.
Morning Meditations

"Welcome every morning with a smile. Let your first hour set the theme of success and positive action that is certain to echo through your entire day."
Og Mandino

Concept for Today

Each morning we rise, ready to face another day. If we can take a minute to read a positive thought first thing each morning, our noisy minds will quiet down and we will have some energy with which to focus. Use this positive thought to cancel out any negativity. There is something amazing about hearing or reading an upbeat message at the start of the day. It unlocks your mind and stays with you. For example, have you ever heard a song in the morning which stays with you? No matter what you do, you just cannot get that song out of your head. Imagine having a positive morning thought ring throughout your mind for the entire day. Repeating an uplifting notion each morning helps your outlook and your day to be optimistic.

In The Classroom

In the classroom, if a stressful or negative thought runs through my mind, I can cancel it out by repeating my optimistic declaration; after all, the brain can only think one thought at a time.

On a Personal Note…

I know that if I train my brain to repeat positive affirmations, they will stick with me and change my thinking. Pick a quote or a line of a song, or a phrase that you like, and repeat it for thirty days. See if your disposition improves.

Action for the Day

- ✓ Today, find a positive statement. Memorize it. Write it down. Then observe yourself throughout the day. Watch what happens when you replace a negative thought with your positive affirmation. Note what emotions emerge. Journal your experience.

6 Seconds Moment

- ◆ Take six seconds to write an affirmation on a post-it and stick it on your mirror.

#63.
Money

"You can only become truly accomplished at something you love. Don't make money your goal. Instead, pursue the things you love doing, and then do them so well that people can't take their eyes off you."
Maya Angelou

Concept for Today

It is a shame that money and a teaching career do not go hand in hand. Teachers should be paid the highest of salaries because the future is literally in their hands, sitting at those desks. I recall reading a book entitled, Do What You Love and the Money Will Follow: Discovering Your Right Livelihood, written by Marsha Sinetar. After reading this book, I learned a valuable life lesson. I must be happy in my career or everything in my life will fail. Fortunately, most teachers enter the profession because they truly love working with kids and want to make a difference. They are not working to become rich, but are working to provide richness to a child's life.

In The Classroom

In the classroom, teachers can set goals to become outstanding educators, hold seminars for others, develop innovative lesson plans, mentor teacher candidates, or write a book. By being passionate about teaching and giving 100% to their craft, the possibilities will follow. For example, I have always been extremely passionate about creativity and curriculum units. I have set a goal to develop an intriguing curriculum class for educators. If I am true and compassionate about utilizing my gifts, my hope is to someday offer this course at a university, community center, adult school, or my district. If I think creatively, there will be opportunities for generating additional income. I cannot be self-seeking or greedy.

On a Personal Note...

For myself, I grew up having a lot of money, but had very little appreciation for it. When I grew older, I experienced having very little money and lots of debt. I had a great deal of guilt about the way I handled money, and had to do some inner, emotional work to release the old patterns. I also had to let go of the huge fear of not having enough. Now, I have a great sense of gratitude for money and continue to increase my respect for it.

Action for the Day

✓ Today, allow yourself to be open to acquiring money. List ways of bringing more money into your life, and write down plans to move forward in the education field.

6 Seconds Moment

◆ Take six seconds to ask which is more important: Unconditional love or an endless bank account?

#64.
Be Gentle But Tough When Making Changes

"I am always doing that which I can not do, in order that I may learn how to do it."
Pablo Picasso

Concept for Today

Life offers us many opportunities to grow and move forward, but change is difficult. For example, I have obsessed about and fought my weight for thirty-three years. I have been on many diets and would beat myself up for binging or gaining weight. I would use food as a comfort and friend, when things were rotten. I would also reward myself with food. I desperately knew that something needed to change. I knew that this continual up and down was dangerous to my health. I decided to attempt another diet. Before I even began, I gave myself time to process the idea. I set a later date when I knew things would be less chaotic to begin the diet.

The first few days were absolutely miserable. I had to be gentle but tough to get through these days. The days passed and the regimen I had instituted became a little easier. I began to see success. Why did this diet work when others had not? One reason is that I was mentally prepared for the change. The second reason was that I was tough with myself, but also loving and gentle at the same time. I was able to lose twenty pounds and keep it off.

In The Classroom

In the classroom, students may struggle with new material. Do not let them give up! Be gentle but tough with them. Find a balance between softness and firmness, so kids can move through tough concepts and learn. They may also kick against the bricks when new rules and expectations are implemented. Remain gentle but tough as well.

On a Personal Note…

For myself, changing my bad habits can be quite challenging. To achieve the positive changes, I must be firm but avoid negative self-reprimands.

Action for the Day

- ✓ Today, think of situations in your life and classroom in which you need to be gentle but tough. Consider any changes you would like to make and write them down for additional reflection.

6 Seconds Moment

- ◆ Take six seconds to think about something you would like to change about yourself. Set a goal and a timeline.

#65.
Essence

"In essence, if we want to direct our lives, we must take control of our consistent actions. It's not what we do once in a while that shapes our lives, but what we do consistently."
Anthony Robbins

Concept for Today

What is your essence? What are you about on a deeper level? What does your real self know and do? We can be so caught up in the day-to-day rat race that we forget who we are inside. The real you may be pure, positive, kind, and thoughtful. Yet our negative belief systems and shortcomings can weigh us down. When we are in our essence, or true self, we do not judge others, act selfishly, or experience guilt. In our essence we are at our highest good. We can tap into our essence by practicing meditation, and forgiving ourselves and others.

In The Classroom

In the classroom, I work to see all students in their essence. I realize that they, like me, have shortcomings, but I am grateful to be in a position to help children reach their authentic selves and extinguish negative behaviors.

On a Personal Note…

I am in my essence when I teach students, plan lessons, or practice creative writing. When are you in your essence?

Action for the Day

✓ Today, make a list of negative behaviors that no longer serve your ultimate goals. Work on a daily basis to shorten your list of shortcomings by making positive changes that will help you to become the real you.

6 Seconds Moment

◆ Take six seconds to write one behavior that no longer serves you. Take another six seconds to determine how you can eliminate that habit.

#66.
Patience

"Have courage for the great sorrows of life and patience for the small ones; and when you have laboriously accomplished your daily task, go to sleep in peace."
Victor Hugo

Concept for Today

How patient are you? Patience is a hard characteristic to practice when angry, overtired, or frustrated. Ask yourself in what areas of your life you are patient. Are there any areas lacking? I have observed that I am more patient with others than with myself.

In The Classroom

In my classroom, I have often been commended for being so patient with my students. My patience with each student is increased when I take "6 seconds" to think before I say something that I may regret. Or take a deep breath, or count to ten, or remove myself from the situation. Also, I can shift my attention by helping another student.

On a Personal Note…

When I lose patience, I know that I am not only hurting others, but hurting myself. By remaining patient, I give and receive gifts of serenity, fortitude, and tolerance.

Action for the Day

- ✓ On a piece of paper, make two columns. In the left column, list areas in your life where you exhibit patience. On the right column, list triggers and areas that may cause you to lose patience.

6 Seconds Moment

- ◆ Take six seconds to step back, re-group, and pick one area upon which to practice patience.

#67.
Pain Eraser

"Pain is inevitable, suffering is optional."
Charles Green

Concept for Today

Everyone has had painful experiences. The question is whether we process them and move forward, or hang onto painful experiences. Perhaps our goal should be to "let go" and thoroughly erase the pain. Time is a great healer. When it comes to your physical body, do you have a strong tolerance for pain, or crumble at the slightest ache or twinge? What do you do for physical hurt? What about emotional discomfort? What is your tolerance level? How do you release the anguish?

In The Classroom

In the classroom, I do believe that painful experiences help us to develop sympathy and compassion. We can empathize with students who experience pain either physically or mentally. Give journal writing prompts to help students handle life's pain. For example, I present a writing lesson on people who have died. I play the Beatles song, "In My Life," and then I ask students to create a tribute for a deceased loved one. The exercise can be very healing.

On a Personal Note...

For myself, I realize that the only way to be completely peaceful is to be rid of past hurts. I do myself a disservice by carrying around old pain in my heart.

Action for the Day

- ✓ Identify and write down types of pain that you are experiencing. Brainstorm options to manage or erase the pain. Also, create a lesson plan for your students to help them deal with emotional pain.

6 Seconds Moment

- ◆ Take six seconds to recognize a painful feeling. Remind yourself that the pain is temporary, and that you have choice.

#68.
A Sprinkle Of Sugar Helps The Medicine Go Down

"Suck on a lollypop after ingesting medicine. It helps get rid of the nasty taste."
Anonymous

Concept for Today

We can accept the challenging times of life more easily when a little sweetness is added. Paying bills, going to the doctor, and housecleaning can be accomplished more effectively and painlessly with a little positive thinking.

Life is composed of both cherries and lemons. Sometimes the lemons turn sour and begin to rot. During dark times and trials, add some cherries to your life. When times seem dark, think about how you would treat a best friend who was feeling this way. Make a decision to treat yourself as kindly. You might get extra rest, cry, exercise, feed your mind with positive inspirational thoughts, or even have that extra helping of chocolate cake. Treat yourself as gently as possible.

When there are annoying errands that need to be completed, or tasks at work that you hate, or long-overdue chores, give yourself one or more cherries. For example, I hate to do the laundry, so I play my favorite music while doing it. If I have to go grocery shopping, I take my daughter with me and we can have a pleasant visit.

In The Classroom

In the classroom, standardized tests are sometimes the yucky medicine that kids have to take. I make the situation as pleasant as possible by reviewing material, building up self-confidence, and reducing the stress. I may even bring in muffins and juice to serve before they take the tests.

On a Personal Note...

There are several things I hate to do, such as cleaning up after my dog, vacuuming, and doing the dishes. I try to make each experience as pleasant as possible by pairing the task with a favorite activity.

Action for the Day

- ✓ Today, write down how you normally treat yourself when you are going through painful life experiences. Are you as gentle with yourself as possible? What can you do to make each task more pleasant?

6 Seconds Moment

- ◆ Take six seconds for a spoonful of positive thinking when completing an unpleasant task.

#69.
Cultural Differences

"Prejudice is the child of ignorance"
William Hazlitt

Concept for Today

As an educator, do you observe your students demonstrating racial profiling, bigotry, and prejudice? We are not only responsible for providing academics, but are required to teach tolerance and acceptance of cultural, racial, and ethnic differences. If there were a magic formula for raising today's youth to be free of prejudice and ingrained social injustice, we could change the world. I do believe that all educators have a common responsibility in teaching students to accept and celebrate individual differences. If we bonded together to do this daily, positive changes would happen more quickly.

In The Classroom

In the classroom, I can make a difference. I observed a colleague present a thought-provoking lesson on hate crimes: A Sikh had experienced nothing but terror, cruelty, and horror for looking like a Muslim. His older brother was murdered and the family terrorized after 9/11. It was a gut-wrenching story that helped the students open their eyes and minds.

On a Personal Note…

For myself, I always use my creativity to teach cultural acceptance and support for all human beings. Every time I work to learn and understand the heritage of others, I grow and appreciate the world so much more.

Action for the Day

✓ Today, think of a lesson on different cultures. Ask yourself if you have any prejudices.

6 Seconds Moment

◆ Take six seconds to say something positive to each member of your class.

#70.
Using Riches

"Riches do not consist in the possession of treasures, but in the use made of them."
Napoleon Bonaparte

Concept for Today

Do you have a favorite piece of jewelry or object that lifts your spirits? Do you carry it with you, especially on stressful days? There is something to be said for objects that bring good thoughts. Do you have any gifts that elevate your moods?

In The Classroom

In the classroom, inanimate objects can have power. I love to place an unusual object in the front of the classroom and let students study it and write about it. This object can be anything; the effect occurs with the imagination and uniqueness with which you present the lesson. Also, I try to remember that special objects and materials improve lessons. For example, I use Euros and Saudi Arabian currency to teach hands-on math. Kids love to manipulate and use real objects.

On a Personal Note…

For myself, I have a little place in my home that is only mine. I keep some of my favorite things there, such as a mini-waterfall, books, and candles. On stressful and anxious days, when I need a lift, I wear a special jewelry piece to remind myself of both my goals and my talents.

Action for the Day

- ✓ Today, bring or wear an object that makes you happy. Think creatively and make a list of objects that can be used in your lessons. Then make a plan to incorporate real objects into your classroom.

6 Seconds Moment

- ◆ Take six seconds to observe three beautiful treasures in your home. Why are they valuable to you? What memories do they conjure up?

#71.
Comfort

"Comfort was allowed to come to them rare, welcome, unsought: a gift like joy."
Ursula K. LeGuin

Concept for Today

When things go wrong in life, or in your classroom, how do you comfort yourself? Do you assure yourself that everything will work out for the best? This is wonderful advice but it is not always practiced. Some people may turn to food, drugs, or alcohol to seek comfort. Others shop. What positive things do you implement to help yourself?

In The Classroom

In the classroom, if you are feeling stressed, how can you immediately comfort yourself? If a student is hurting and in need of self-comfort, what are your tools for assisting him/her? What self-soothing tools do you teach?

On a Personal Note...

I admit it; there are still times that I use chocolate for comfort. However, my usual rituals for comforting myself are to talk to a loved one, have a good cry, or tune out and watch a good movie. I also find comfort by reading a good book, walking my dog, or attending church.

Action for the Day

✓ Today, write down three thoughts that will comfort you in stressful situations. Try repeating, "Everything is working for my highest good," "This too shall pass, or "I love myself and I am safe."

6 Seconds Moment

◆ Take six seconds to provide comfort to yourself by massaging your neck.

#72.
Crisis

"Man is not imprisoned by habit. Great changes in him can be wrought by crisis–once that crisis can be recognized and understood."
Norman Cousins

Concept for Today

Experiencing a crisis is very painful, upsetting, and can feel almost unbearable. A major crisis can rip our souls to shreds if we allow it. When going through an emotionally stressful event or traumatic change in life, what do your coping skills look like? What is your own process for dealing with a crisis situation? When there is a major crisis in life, such as a death of a loved one, you will go through several stages, experiencing grief, denial, anger, and finally acceptance. How much time you will remain in these phases is unknown. It is important not to stay stuck.

In The Classroom

In the classroom, my first permanent job as a teacher's aide was working with pre-school children in wheelchairs. The teacher, named Mary, was an absolutely delightful person with a heart of gold. Six months into the job, she was diagnosed with breast cancer. Our educational staff was broken-hearted and worried about Mary. She went through chemotherapy, lost her hair, and was absent for two months. The doctor told her to take it easy; however, Mary came back to work. She said that work would keep her mind off of her cancer and lift her spirits. It has now been ten years and Mary is still teaching little children in wheelchairs.

On a Personal Note…

I have a major fear of losing my beloved grandmother. She is still alive, but I fear the time when she dies. I used to think that when that happened I would lose my will to live. Thank goodness, there are options for coping, such as grief counseling, or therapy. Another coping tool is helping others less fortunate than I. I don't know exactly how well I will cope when this crisis hits, but I do know that I won't let it kill me emotionally.

Action for the Day

- ✓ Today, write down your coping skills for handling a major crisis in your life.

6 Seconds Moment

- ◆ Take six seconds to tell yourself that you are a champion survivor in any situation.

#73. Places

"Our first journey is to find that special place for us."
Earl Nightingale

Concept for Today

Throughout your life, has there ever been a place to which you have been especially drawn? You may have seen this place in a movie, in your dreams, or read about it. If you could go anywhere in the world, where would you go? It is important never to forget this beautiful place and make a decision to visit it.

In The Classroom

In the classroom, I love teaching world geography. My hope is to open the door to possibilities of travel, different scenery, and a diverse way of life. It is extraordinarily helpful to plant visions of beauty, uniqueness, and grandeur in the minds of my students. It was shocking to me to discover, when I taught a unit on the Golden Gate Bridge to my Bay Area students to discover that many had never seen or crossed the amazing structure.

It occurred to me that my students had never been out of their own neighborhoods. I immediately planned a field trip for students to walk across the Golden Gate Bridge. The trip was an astounding success, as well as something that students will remember forever.

On a Personal Note…

I have always dreamed of living on the East coast. My special place is Nantucket. I actually think about retiring there. Of course, a trip or permanent stay would take planning, but the fact is that I will not stomp on my dream. We must keep dreaming, no matter our age. Personal dreams keep the fire in our souls burning.

Action for the Day

- ✓ Today, think about the place that you would most like to see. Research your special place, and write about it. Affirm your dream by finding some pictures of it and setting aside time to start making plans to visit.

6 Seconds Moment

- ◆ Take six seconds to affirm that you will begin research on your special place.

#74.
High Vibrational Thought

"Everything in this world has a vibration. Every emotion that you can think of has a vibration. Love is a very special, very uplifting vibration."
Amma Sri Karunamyi

Concept for Today

Often we are so busy running to meet daily demands, so overloaded with menial day-to-day tasks that we forget to think consciously. When we are at peace, centered and connected to nature, or in a meditative state, we can, in fact, reach a higher vibrational thought. Remember that these thoughts can be used to make a difference in our lives, as well as the lives of others. When we are relaxed, we think more clearly and can tap into our intuition.

We have all experienced higher vibrational thinking at one time or another in our lives. These are the times when we just know that we have a special purpose, or that we made the right decision from which all will benefit.

In The Classroom

In the classroom, many teachers are intuitive. Are you a better teacher when relaxed, open to higher thinking, and connected? Or, when you are frazzled, tired, and short tempered? Practice higher vibrational thinking by stopping the mundane, becoming aware of your senses, taking a few deep breaths, opening up your consciousness, and asking for what you need for the day. Apply this process when you have a tough decision to make, and then be open to the solutions that come.

On a Personal Note...

For myself, life flows with ease and grace when I practice the concept of higher vibrational thinking. With this type of belief I am able to reach my full potential.

Action for the Day

- ✓ Today, ask yourself, "What do I need to know for this day?" Write down what practices might help you to become more aware of the world around you.

6 Seconds Moment

- ♦ Take six seconds to take a breath and observe your thoughts. Are you connected or scattered? Make a conscious decision to free your mind from anxiety and listen to your intuitive voice.

#75.
One Thing

"Catch yourself doing something right today."
Aline Kaprive

Concept for Today

Teaching can be a rough business. It can wring you dry. It can take everything out of you. On top of this, things may be a struggle in your personal life. This can add up to anxiety, burn-out, and chaos. However, if we can remind ourselves of one thing in our daily lives or in the classroom that has been successful, we can once again gain strength.

In The Classroom

In the classroom, if I can grab onto something that is a desired outcome, it will boost my morale, alter my mood from negative to positive, and give me the courage to persevere. There have been many days in my career when I felt sad, tired, and unenthusiastic. However, during these episodes, I kept my eyes open and grabbed onto one thing that went right. For example, I used to work with students who were wheelchair-bound. One little girl who had cerebral palsy greeted me each day with a great, big smile, no matter what. This was the one thing that kept me going and gave my heart cheer. Even though this little girl faced severe challenges, she was always able to greet me with a grin.

On a Personal Note…

For myself, I am happier during the worst of days as long as I can grab onto and remember one thing that was successful.

Action for the Day

- ✓ Today, keep your eyes open for an unexpected break that you might receive, or for that one thing that goes right. This can alter your mood.

6 Seconds Moment

- ◆ Take six seconds to consciously say that you deserve things to go right in your life, and that things will get better.

#76.
May The Power Be With You

"Each of us is born with the potential for unfolding of our true self. When you deviate from the truth, you are interfering with the intention of something greater than you are dealt; call it nature or a higher power. As a result, you develop discomfort."
Anonymous

Concept for Today

In the Star Wars series created by George Lucas, the characters say, "May the Force be with You." Each individual has his or her own beliefs regarding religion, a higher power, or spirituality. Some people may not be religious, but are spiritual. Some people believe in karma, some in the power of positive thinking. Some people are agnostics or atheists. Any stance should be respected. Place value on who you are and pay tribute to your beliefs. The key is to have a lifeline, or connection to something greater than ourselves upon which to rely. What are your personal beliefs?

In The Classroom

In the classroom, we are told to keep church and state separate. The only time in the classroom that I may touch this delicate subject is when I teach World Religion. I value all children no matter their religion and try on a daily basis to be sensitive to each student's beliefs.

On a Personal Note…

I am both religious and spiritual. I need to believe in something greater than myself. Life can become so difficult at times that it is a relief to know that something like the Force, something powerful and positive, is with me no matter what obstacle comes my way. I like to believe that I am being watched over, guided, and protected and that my concerns are addressed. I keep my ears open for wisdom, love, and guidance. I never want to feel alone on the road of life.

Action for the Day

- ✓ Today, ask yourself about your beliefs and spiritual practices. How do you care for yourself on a spiritual level? Ask yourself if you are open to new ideas. Write down your beliefs and take an inventory of your spiritual health. Ask yourself if you feel loved, protected, and guided by a force more powerful than yourself.

6 Seconds Moment

- ◆ Take six seconds to say, "The force is with me, and I will have a beautiful, rewarding day."

#77.
A Beverly Hillbillies Moment

"It is sweet to let the mind unbend on occasion."
Horace

Concept for Today

Do you remember that silly comedy, "The Beverly Hillbillies" created by Paul Henning? During the 1960's and early 70's the United States was at war in Northern Vietnam. People needed an emotional break. The networks aired silly TV shows to take our minds off of the atrocities overseas. Our minds needed a time out. Do you practice relieving your mind from the horrors of the war, global warming, famine, recession, and injustice? What is your daily attitude? Grant yourself permission to relieve your mind of the mayhem. Take a time out and watch a silly show. Find a way to add laughter to your regular rituals.

In The Classroom

In the classroom, as teachers, we are faced with more challenges than ever before. We need to teach students to find courage to handle their fear and empower them to believe that they are capable of making a difference in the world. We want students to be aware but not afraid. To lighten heavy curriculums, incorporate a funny movie or TV show. Give the kids a break. For example, in mathematics, I have shown cartoons that teach probability and algebra. A little research can provide many lighter ways to teach core subjects and issues of today.

On a Personal Note...

For myself, when I can rise above the pain and suffering of the world and be willing to help those around me then I can find true peace. Can you find serenity during these turbulent times?

Action for the Day

✓ Today, be aware of, but not controlled by, the heartbreaks of the world. Make a change in your daily routine and don't watch the news before bed. Write down five ways that you could teach students to prepare for the future. Write down one way that you teach core academics with a lighter touch.

6 Seconds Moment

◆ Take six seconds to remind yourself that you are preparing students for the future.

#78. Boundaries

"Establishing healthy, personal boundaries is not a selfish act, but a requirement for a happier existence."
Aline Kaprive

Concept for Today

It can be very draining to help the kids who are in so much need. It can be even more exhausting to meet the needs of co-workers and supervisors. We are in the profession of helping, giving, listening, and responding to others. If we do not set consistent boundaries, we may become a dried up well, with nothing left to contribute. Boundaries set a safety zone between giving to others and protecting our own emotional well-being. Where do you draw the line? By knowing yourself and your own needs, you can set boundaries that allow you to give help and support without depleting your energy. Do you set aside time each day for replenishing your own emotional and physical energy? Think of what your personal boundaries need to be and respect them.

In The Classroom

In the classroom, it is important to set boundaries with students. For example, you would never allow a student to strike you, or call you names, or consume so much of your time that you have nothing left to give other students. What about the demands of your supervisor or co-workers? Can you say, "No," in an assertive manner? If we are consumed with thoughts of everyone else's needs, it is difficult to make a difference with our students.

On a Personal Note...

For myself, I have often been labeled as a doormat, or wishy-washy. I compromised my boundaries and needs. Now, I realize that it is perfectly reasonable to say "No," as long as I say it with respect for the other person.

Action for the Day

- ✓ Today, evaluate your boundaries inside and outside the classroom. Maybe your boundaries are too rigid. The ultimate goal is to replenish your own energy, so you can be the most accommodating for your students. Evaluate your boundaries throughout all relationships in your life. Ask yourself, "Do I remember to care for myself before others?"

6 Seconds Moment

- ◆ Take six seconds to remind yourself that you have parameters that help you to be a replenished and unique individual.

#79.
Permission

"When you take charge of your life, there is no longer need to ask permission of other people or society at large. When you ask permission, you give someone veto power over your life."
Albert F. Geoffrey

Concept for Today

How often do you seek permission? Some people do not grant themselves permission to enjoy the precious things in life such as time off, fun, spontaneous events, eating junk food, or a quick nap. We can push ourselves into being "human doings," who must always be performing something constructive or worthwhile. Even more significant is the fact that some of us do not grant ourselves permission to "be." Where did we learn that permission is so necessary in day-to-day life? I grew up with a strict, military-type father. I had to ask permission for every little thing. As a result, I did not make my own decisions until I grew older and strengthened my self-esteem.

In The Classroom

What is your permission policy? Do students need to ask permission to use the restroom, speak, or get up to sharpen a pencil? Permission may be necessary; it shows respect for the teacher and other students. Evaluate your permission policy. Is it too harsh or too weak? Do you grant students permission to share their thoughts, ideas and creativity? Are students allowed to have opinions? Are they allowed to share more than one way of problem solving or thinking?

On a Personal Note...

For myself, I need to grant myself permission to really enjoy life and not sweat the small stuff.

Action for the Day

- ✓ Today, grant yourself permission to either do something you wouldn't normally do or to skip something you usually do. Write down your permission policy for your classroom, and most importantly for yourself. Ask yourself if you are granting yourself permission to be who you really are, and also if you're giving students permission to be their authentic selves.

6 Seconds Moment

- ◆ Take six seconds to grant yourself permission to do something fun today.

#80.
Slates And Chalkboards

"I CAN is 100 times more important than IQ."
Anonymous

Concept for Today

Remember the old-fashioned slates and chalkboards? In the twenty-first century we no longer utilize these. We know chalk dust is hazardous to our health, so we now use whiteboards in our meeting rooms and classrooms. Through past mistakes and experiences we are always making improvements. No more chalk dust for us!

Each person has an invisible chalkboard in the brain where they store experiences, thoughts, and life's data. Some people's chalkboards are overloaded with negative junk which they no longer need. What are some of the messages written on your slate?

In The Classroom

In the classroom, I post a rule that there are no put-downs allowed. This goes for self-criticism as well. To eliminate the put-downs and negativity, I teach an emotionally intelligent lesson called, "Put-Down Burial." I have students write down all of the put-downs which they have heard throughout their lives and then ask them to identify some of the feelings they experienced hearing them. We then compose a poster with all put-downs illustrated; then we rip it up, and throw it away. This is a lesson which helps students reduce future negative comments.

On a Personal Note…

I enjoy doing a visualization activity in my mind. I begin with deep breathing and getting comfortable. I picture a whiteboard and write down all of the put-downs that I have heard while growing up, and the casual ones I lay upon myself. I then visualize a giant eraser and wipe the board clean. Finally, I fill the board with positive comments.

Action for the Day

- ✓ Today, wipe your slate clean. Write down five negative self put-downs and erase them. Fill your slate with positive, upbeat, and optimistic thoughts.

6 Seconds Moment

- ♦ Take six seconds to say something kind and loving about you! Take another six seconds to give yourself a pat on the back.

#81.
Fire In Your Belly

"Blaze with the fire that is never extinguished"
Luisa Sigea

Concept for Today

We are educators and have a true passion for helping kids to learn and succeed. We have fire in our bellies. There is a thrill when it comes to tapping into our hunger for teaching. We need to remember that we will always have fire and gusto when it comes to teaching. It is who we are.

In The Classroom

Remember why you went into teaching. I recall one of the key reasons that I wanted to teach was because I hoped to deliver a significant and meaningful education to all students. I wanted to do this by presenting lessons that students would enjoy and remember. I especially wanted the low-achieving kids and those struggling with dyslexia, to fall in love with learning and master the material.

On a Personal Note...

For myself, I know that I am strong. I am fiery and passionate and have many gifts to give. Even on days when I feel discouraged, I can remember that my passion and love for teaching is embedded in my roots. It is who I am.

Action for the Day

✓ Today, count the ways that you have passion and fire in your belly regarding teaching. What would you do if someone said, "You cannot teach anymore because you drill and kill your students and are boring them to death!" Write a response to this.

6 Seconds Moment

◆ Take six seconds to shout that you are a powerful, fiery, and effervescent teacher.

#82.
College Graduate

"You have brains in your head. You have feet in your shoes. You can steer yourself in any direction you choose. You're on your own. And you know what you know. You are the guy who'll decide where to go."
Dr. Seuss

Concept for Today

Do you ever think about being a college graduate? Do you ever pat yourself on the back for your accomplishments? Graduating college is a huge accomplishment not to be taken lightly, or forgotten. Do you remember when you received your degree? How did it make you feel? What about the additional hoops that you jumped through to earn your teaching credential? Be proud of yourself, and never forget your own educational experience. It will strengthen your teaching.

In The Classroom

In the classroom, I work diligently to provide a quality education and help students to attain their potential. I also model and teach study skills throughout the curriculum. Periodically, I will share my college experience and how much I wanted to become a teacher. Students love it! I also have seen teachers who have their graduation pictures framed and placed on their desks, as well as their high school yearbooks on hand. Let students know that you were once a student.

On a Personal Note…

I still have dreams of furthering my education. I also envision becoming a college professor. I recognize the work and energy this will require. Do you have any educational dreams?

Action for the Day

✓ Today, reflect upon your educational past. What was positive and what was negative? Do you have any special memories? Recall details and write a summary of your own experience.

6 Seconds Moment

◆ Take six seconds to remember the day you graduated college and how you felt. Take the joy into your day of teaching.

#83.
Forward Thinking

"The 'how' thinker gets problems solved effectively because he wastes no time with futile 'ifs'."
Norman Vincent Peale

Concept for Today

What kind of a thinker are you? Are you visionary, open, and using all eight of your intelligences? Are you an introverted contemplator or extroverted mover and shaker? Do you think about your future or past? Do you use more than one method to solve a problem? Do you think about beauty, art, nature, and music? Are you a creative thinker, or set in your ways? Do you look at life from different angles? Are you an "out of the box" thinker? Are you analytical or a free flowing thinker? Do you think critically? Are you a seeker or investigator? Do you question the status quo?

In The Classroom

In the classroom, it is extremely valuable to encourage and help students develop multiple processes for thinking. I love to have students think critically and scientifically, as well as artistically and creatively. Since children are so unique, establish different ways to assess your students, such as essays, art, multiple-choice questions, and work samples utilizing a variety of methods, including media tools.

On a Personal Note...

I value my own unique thinking procedure. I know that when learning new material, I need to process it slowly. Sometimes, I need to sleep on things. I also need to write down items (tactile reinforcement) to help solidify the material. Each week, I work on finding different thinking techniques.

Action for the Day

- ✓ Today, ask yourself what your thinking process is. Decide whether you are field-dependent or field-independent. How distracted are you by the environment?

6 Seconds Moment

- ♦ Take six seconds to identify someone who thinks very differently from you. Have a conversation with them about a controversial topic. What did you learn?

#84.
Boredom

"Boredom: the desire for desires."
Leo Tolstoy

Concept for Today

What do you do when you are bored? How do you feel when things are dull and tiresome? Have you ever had a boring job? What do you do if you have to wait in a long line? Do you ever get restless with the day-to-day monotony? Are your weekends always filled with housecleaning, laundry, grocery shopping, and running errands?

One day while walking my dog, I met a teacher, a sixteen-year veteran, and asked her about her work. She told me it was always the same. She was already exhausted even though it was only September.

Pretend that you have been teaching that long. You have your set curriculum. There are no surprises. What if you added three new units that you have never taught before? How would you feel?

I might feel a little anxious but would hope the new material would be successful. By exploring new strategies and engaging in different learning modalities and lessons, boredom leaves me and I am set free from the doldrums.

In The Classroom

What do you notice when students are bored? There may be more talking, disruptive behavior, and chaos. Think about your own past experience. Who was the most boring teacher that you ever had? Did they smother you with drill and kill lessons, dry lectures, and extensive busy work packets? Did you learn from this person? Have you ever had a teacher who got carried away with his or her lectures and loved to hear their own monotone voice?

On a Personal Note...

Boredom has gotten me into trouble. I discovered that over-eating takes away boredom. Crankiness also accompanies boredom. So, I have some set activities to help myself when bored. I can go to the gym, I can sit in the sauna, I can go to the library, or I can call a friend.

Action for the Day

- ✓ Today, what can you do to get rid of boredom in your own life? What advice would you give to my friend who has been teaching English for sixteen years?

6 Seconds Moment

- ◆ Take six seconds to think of something exciting that you would like to do.

#85.
Calendars

"First comes thought; then organization of that thought, into ideas and plans; then transformation of those plans into reality. The beginning, as you will observe, is in your imagination."
Napoleon Hill

Concept for Today

In today's fast-paced world, we usually write things down on a calendar or an electronic device of some type. Calendars help our brains to keep track of things. Have you ever lost your calendar? I remember in the 1980's that my mother had a big calendar book which she carried everywhere. She called it her "brain" and had it filled to capacity. The teaching profession takes a great deal of time, so we must not over-fill our calendars. Sometimes, we have to say, "No!" So, go ahead and plan your calendars, but make them your friend and not your master.

In The Classroom

In the classroom, students benefit from using a calendar to help them plan, organize, and remember when assignments are due. I like to not only provide calendars to remind students of when assignments need to be completed, but also to break down the assignments into separate, distinct tasks. For example, I taught a unit on nutrition. At the end of the unit, students were required to write a paper and make a poster. I put the due dates, but also included dates for when the rough draft of the paper was due, and the ideas for the poster. This way my students were not rushing at the last minute to complete the final assignments.

On a Personal Note...

For myself, I use a calendar and a lesson plan book. Writing things down relieves a lot of stress. I like to break projects down into manageable tasks.

Action for the Day

✓ Today, ask yourself what your calendar looks like. Does keeping a calendar help you? Evaluate your method and determine if you are "over" or "under" doing it. Provide a calendar for your students.

6 Seconds Moment

◆ Take six seconds to check your current calendar. Is it up to date? Is there a future event for which you should begin planning?

#86.
Stillness

"Your innermost sense of self, of who you are, is inseparable from stillness. This is the "I AM" that is deeper than name and form."
Eckhart Tolle

Concept for Today

Do you ever sit and listen to the stillness? Do you incorporate quiet time into your daily life? How often do you have a little quiet time just for yourself? Find a time throughout your day to just be calm and silent. This can be accomplished each day by taking five minutes to simply stop and relax. Please find the time to give your brain and emotions some time off.

In The Classroom

In the classroom, also work to find quiet time. It may be at the beginning of lunch, after students are dismissed, or before class begins. You can find quietness in a library, or when students are doing the practice section of an assignment. To help my students quiet down, I stand at the door to greet them each morning, and ask them to come into the room quietly. I also softly play music to set a soothing atmosphere. Students need their own quiet time. When presenting lessons, I use Powerpoint presentations with cool color print that prepares students for the upcoming activity whether it is low-talking with collaboration, partner work, or quiet, independent study.

On a Personal Note…

For myself, I need my down time each day to produce tranquil thoughts. If I grant myself quiet time, I am a more patient and welcoming individual. My family and students benefit.

Action for the Day

- ✓ Today, calm down and be still. Identify how you can achieve peacefulness and quietness in your own life as well as in your classroom.

6 Seconds Moment

- ◆ Take six seconds to just be still several times today.

#87.
Sweets And Treats

"Pleasure is eating chocolate."
Anonymous

Concept for Today

The USDA states that we should use fats, oils, and sweets sparingly. Don't worry so much about "shoulds" and "supposed-to's". Go ahead and enjoy a little treat now and then. Take pleasure in the little delights in life and savor them slowly. Moderation is the key, so go ahead and have that one piece of candy– guilt free.

In The Classroom

In the classroom, students love treats. Evaluate how often you dispense goodies. Remember that fruit is nature's candy, so you can also use this. Do you have classroom parties with goodies? One special treat that I love to give students is bottled sparkling water, without sugar or caffeine. They love the water and value it whether I give it to them for exemplary behavior, or "out of the blue" for just being my students. I do this if the class in general, has a wonderful week. The key is moderation combined with surprise.

On a Personal Note…

I do treat myself occasionally to goodies. There is a time for extra treats, and a time to prevent over-indulgences.

Action for the Day

- ✓ Today, go ahead and indulge a little. Give permission to yourself to splurge.

6 Seconds Moment

- ◆ Take six seconds to have a piece of candy. Take another six seconds to identify why this is a pleasure.

#88.
Kind-Heartedness

"If you haven't any charity in your heart, you have the worst kind of heart trouble."
Bob Hope

Concept for Today

Sometimes the world is not kind. Therefore, grab onto the kindnesses given to you and remember the kindnesses that you have given. If we are kind with ourselves we can be kind to others. Can you think of someone in your life that has always shown you kindness? What types of kindness do you give to others? Kindness is a powerful act which creates ripple effects, like throwing a pebble into a calm pond. What are you doing to increase the ripples?

In The Classroom

In the classroom, we must be kind-hearted towards all students. Practice kindness at all times and observe what happens. Do you know about random acts of kindness? This is when you do something nice for someone else without expecting anything in return. Start your day off by sharing a random act of kindness that you have done. Then ask your students to do the same. Make this a ritual in your classroom because kindness makes way for trust.

On a Personal Note…

For myself, I try to be as kind as possible. I care for others, and I want people to know how special they are to me. I am not sure if it is appropriate or inappropriate, but I do give money to homeless people on the streets. I really surprise them when I hand them a five dollar bill.

Action for the Day

- ✓ Today, rate yourself on kindness. Do you provide regular random acts of kindness? Think of a way to incorporate more kindness into your classroom. Remember that kindness is contagious.

6 Seconds Moment

- ◆ Take six seconds to think of or perform a random act of kindness.

#89. Childhood Innocence

"Every child is an artist. The problem is how to remain an artist once we grow up."
Pablo Picasso

Concept for Today

What have you been doing to keep your childhood innocence alive? Do you remember activities you enjoyed when you were a child? Do you recall making wishes on the "poof balls" of dandelions?

In The Classroom

In the classroom, most children arrive with the qualities of imagination, enthusiasm, inquisitiveness, and anticipation. We can tap into these qualities, and revive curiosity. Some children may have lost their innocence due to an abusive home, divorce, violence, and neglect.

In the classroom, how do we help these children to rediscover their creativity, imagination, and enthusiasm? First, we offer structure, consistency, love, security and safety. By establishing a strong trusting relationship with our wounded students, we are sowing the seeds of safety and security. Once safety and trust are established, we can introduce lessons that will enhance their thinking, and encourage their creativity. We can also add social and emotional intelligence lessons to build empathy and optimism. I enjoy showing a movie that may have been a childhood favorite during times of innocence. When my kids watched "The NeverEnding Story" directed by Wolfgang Petersen they were moved to tears when the horse got stuck and was left to die in the quicksand. Their childhood purity was deeply touched.

On a Personal Note...

I search for times when I can tap into my childhood excitement and naiveté. Recently, I traveled to Las Vegas and visited the wave pool. I tackled those waves as if I were eight-years old again. As a result, I laughed out loud with joy.

Action for the Day

✓ Today, think of things that will bring out your childhood wonder and joy. Laugh and play, as if you are a child. How can you help your students to keep their childhood innocence alive?

6 Seconds Moment

◆ Take six seconds to think about a favorite activity that gives you joy. Set a goal to do it with a friend.

#90.
Esteemed Friendships

"The better part of one's life consists of his friendships."
Abraham Lincoln

Concept for Today

Consistent friends are a precious gift. What would we do without our special friends? They are there for us through thick and thin and truly want the best for us. Do you remember your first best friend from childhood? What was so special and unique about this individual? How about the friends that you have today? What are their gifts? What are your gifts that you offer your friends? Do you feel renewed and fulfilled when you spend time with them? Get togethers with special friends are a fabulous emotional energizer. For your own well-being, make time in your busy schedule for your treasured friendships.

In The Classroom

It is always interesting to observe the type of friendships that your students forge with one another. As teachers, we want to help students strengthen their empathy skills. What do you do when a student is alienated, or picked on? How about the loner student or new kid? Can you help him or her to establish friendships and to feel accepted? Think about supportive practices you could initiate.

On a Personal Note…

For myself, for a moment of joy, I reflect upon my friendships throughout the years. There have been many unique experiences. No matter what, I will still plan times for friends.

Action for the Day

✓ Today, evaluate what type of friend you are, and write down these characteristics. Review how often you spend quality time with special people in your life. Plan a get-together for friends.

6 Seconds Moment

◆ Take six seconds to tell a friend how much you appreciate his/her care and concern.

#91.
Mini-Mind Relaxants

"This art of resting the mind and the power of dismissing from it all care and worry is probably one of the secrets of energy in our great men."
Captain J. A. Hadfield

Concept for Today

It is very empowering to try and improve one's life. We can accomplish this by exercising, making positive choices, eating right, getting a good night's sleep, meditating, breaking habits and so forth. Perhaps at this point in our life, we are reading good literature and finding fifteen minutes to meditate. We may be practicing positive thinking more frequently. It is time to bring our good practices into our work days.

In The Classroom

I have observed that students read everything posted on the walls. For example, inspirational posters, word walls, standards, regularly changing quotes, and banners capture students' undivided attention. To celebrate your students, post their work. Kids love this. Give them an assignment to create something that will inspire someone else.

On a Personal Note...

Last year after winter break, I had been feeling very "stuck". I desperately wanted a lift during each teaching day. As a gift, I received a tiny book with positive life quotes. For some strange reason, this little book got placed inside my lesson plan book, and came to work with me. I placed the book in my locker, and every time I would go to my locker, there it sat. I found myself reading it during breaks, before school, and at lunchtime. I was giving myself a mini-mind relaxer. My attitude began to improve and I found myself slowing down and thinking positively during the hectic teaching day.

Action for the Day

✓ Today, find a tiny, mini-lift book. Bring it to work and read something each day. Evaluate your room and see if the walls read positively! Commit to yourself a mini-mind relaxant during your chaotic day.

6 Seconds Moment

◆ Take six seconds to relax your mind by thinking of an adage you learned when growing up, such as "Actions Speak Louder than Words."

#92.
Destiny

"Dreams are like stars...you may never touch them, but if you follow them they will lead you to your destiny."
Anonymous

Concept for Today

Throughout history there have been many thoughts, questions, and views regarding one's destiny. Do you believe that each person has a unique destiny? What is yours? Since you are probably in the teaching profession, part of your destiny is to transform and improve the lives of our future generations. Flash back and reflect upon your life thus far. Look at the significant events and recall how you got to where you are today. What brought you into teaching? How did you get into your current assignment?

In The Classroom

In the classroom, each unique child has his or her own life experiences, joys, sorrows, and lessons from which to grow. Value each child and offer him/her encouragement to explore, think, and dream. Remember that you are a guide as well as teacher in the classroom, and help your students to build and cherish their dream. If you teach little children, ask them what they want to be when they grow up. No matter the age, have them draw a picture and give it to their parents as a keepsake. If you teach older children, have them fill out interest inventories regarding career possibilities. Have individual conferences with them regarding their hopes and plans for the future. Encourage students to contemplate their future.

On a Personal Note...

When I was in high school, I never considered teaching or working with children. I thought my destiny was to be a psychologist helping adults. However, at nineteen, a friend advised me to go and apply for the recreation department working as a day camp leader. I took a chance and filled out the application. Two weeks later, I knew that this was the greatest job on earth. If someone had told me six months earlier that I would someday work with children, I never would have believed it.

Action for the Day

- ✓ Today, define your destiny. If you left the earth today, would you be remembered? Are there any changes you need to make to ensure your destiny?

6 Seconds Moment

- ♦ Take six seconds to remind yourself that you are creating destiny each day.

#93.
The Joy Of Life

"Joy is a net of love by which you can catch souls."
Mother Teresa

Concept for Today

How often does one truly enjoy life each and every day? Do you recall experiencing more joy as a child? Sometimes in life there are periods of monotony. At other times, a mountain of obstacles and troubles comes crashing down. Affixed amidst the boredom and tumultuous times, there will also be times of great joy. We need to grab onto the delightful moments and build upon them.

In The Classroom

I enjoy teaching the Declaration of Independence. One of the key points in this document is that all men and women have the right to the pursuit of happiness. Why is happiness mentioned in the Declaration of Independence? Do we have a responsibility to create happiness? Happiness does not just come and stay with us each and every day, but drifts away when problems arise. If happiness is lost, how is it regained?

On a Personal Note...

I remember to hang on so that life may surprise me with a burst of energy and an unexpected treasure. For example, my boss called me in the office and closed the door. She asked me how I would like to be interviewed by the local newspaper regarding my teaching experience in Juvenile Hall. I was so happy and honored. I was beaming with pride. I carried this pleasure with me, observed that my energy was up, and shared it with others.

Action for the Day

✓ Today, recall a joyous experience and write about it. Remember that you are here to pursue happiness and recall that life can change for the better.

6 Seconds Moment

◆ Take six seconds to think of a really happy time in your life. Share this experience with a friend or loved one.

#94. Patterns

"Anyone can live heroically and successfully for one day. The man who achieves a high purpose makes that day the pattern for all the days of his life."
Anonymous

Concept for Today

When I was working toward my teaching credential, one of the requirements was to write my philosophy regarding the teaching of history. One profound answer was that we study history in order to break negative patterns or learn from our mistakes. Do you have certain behavioral patterns that need to be changed? What about habits? A good professor told me that in the teaching profession, it would be a wise idea to switch classroom assignments after each five-year period. One of my worst fears is being in my mid-sixties teaching the same material and using the same methods that I use today in my twelfth year of teaching.

In The Classroom

In the classroom, we must evaluate our teaching patterns, break the costly ones, and not get too comfortable. We need to stretch ourselves and reach for the stars. We must remain open to the development of new patterns. Encourage your students to evaluate their patterns as well. Help them identify the costs and benefits of their various choices and actions.

On a Personal Note...

I have several negative set behavioral patterns, such as repeatedly accusing, stuffing angry feelings, practicing self-pity, and holding grudges. I also have positive patterns, such as caring for others, listening, practicing empathy, walking if I am upset, and searching for new teaching ideas. To grow as a human being, I must acknowledge my own patterns and be willing to incorporate new patterns. Self-observing and willingness to change is half the battle when it comes to changing life-long patterns.

Action for the Day

- ✓ Today, allow yourself to be open to releasing patterns that no longer serve you. Make a list of positive patterns which you possess and also write down patterns that need to be broken.

6 Seconds Moment

- ♦ Take six seconds to remind yourself of a negative pattern that you have broken–and that is no longer encumbering your progress.

#95.
Perpetual Triumph

"Although there may be tragedy in your life, there's always a possibility to triumph. It doesn't matter who you are, where you come from. The ability to triumph begins with you. Always."
Oprah Winfrey

Concept for Today

Even after being a teacher for twelve years, I can honestly say that I have not learned everything about my job. But I do have triumphs each year, and I record them so I will remember. I am perpetually seeking triumphs in my positions as teacher, friend, mother, wife, and daughter. I like to reflect upon situations in which I feel successful.

In The Classroom

In the classroom, I have experienced this type of triumph and success with a few students. For me, perpetual triumph can be measured through various student achievements. Examples would be watching a Juvenile Hall student graduate, helping a second-language learner master English, teaching a dyslexic student to read, or helping a student develop emotional intelligence by maintaining his anger. When a student is successful in his or her own life, I know that I have achieved perpetual triumph. When a student successfully reaches a goal with my help, I know that I have also achieved a personal success.

On a Personal Note...

For myself, I strive to be perpetually triumphant in all areas of my life. I can experience this with life-changing victories, acquiring thoughts and behaviors that will better suit my goals, or being a glorious wife and mother and, most importantly, reaching my potential.

Action for the Day

- ✓ Today, think about your triumphs. Now dig deeper and think about the triumphs that you have generated. Write down the triumphs you would like to have later in life. Remember, a perpetual triumph could be beating cancer, truly loving yourself, letting go of your daily resentments, or practicing conscious acts of kindness.

6 Seconds Moment

- ♦ Take six seconds to plan how you might be triumphant for today.

#96.
Rituals

"Rituals are important. Nowadays it's hip not to be married. I'm not interested in being hip."
John Lennon

Concept for Today

What are the customs or rituals of your life? Do you eat dinner with your family every night? How about Sunday breakfasts? Do you have a quiet-time ritual to rejuvenate your spirit? Is there a special ritual that you do when it comes to paying bills? Even less amusing tasks can be completed with set rituals that are pleasant. On Sundays, my family has a pleasant dinner together and, every three to four months, I have a ritual getaway with girlfriends. Even small rituals such as kissing your family members before you leave for the day can add warmth and sunshine to your life. Or saying "I love you," at the end of a phone call.

In The Classroom

In the classroom, it is equally important to have daily rituals. Examples include morning check-in and journaling, greeting students at the door, writing a reflection at the end of the day, and having students share a joke or random act of kindness. With positive rituals, a safe classroom environment is developed and students are able to relax into a consistent routine that also helps elevate moods.

On a Personal Note…

For myself, it is sometimes challenging to establish and follow through with new rituals. I stay open to possibilities and work to stretch myself. I try to incorporate a new ritual each semester. My latest ritual is going to the movies with co-workers once a month.

Action for the Day

✓ Today, write down your daily and monthly rituals for yourself and your classroom. Think of two new rituals that you would like to incorporate. Ask yourself how rituals help you, as well as your family and students.

6 Seconds Moment

◆ Take six seconds to add a mini-ritual to your day, such as reading an affirmation or quote, smiling at all co-workers, or giving yourself an extra five minutes at the beginning of the school day for establishing goals.

#97.
Silver Linings

"Clouds may come, and clouds may go, and they all have a silver lining. For behind each cloud you know, the sun, or moon, is shining."
Anonymous

Concept for Today

It was the worst day ever! Due to budget cuts, I was given a new teaching assignment for the upcoming school year. I was filled with sorrow. People kept telling me to be grateful that I would still be employed. When my boss notified me that the teacher replacing me wanted to visit my heart ached, but I told the principal I would be gracious. I planned an excellent lesson, and decided that when the new teacher came, I would focus on my beloved kids and their learning.

At the end of the class, she had some questions. I then took a risk and let her know how I felt. I told her that I absolutely loved my job and was very sad to leave my kids. She looked at me with surprise and said, "I was told that you were leaving this job because you were offered a better teaching position. There is no way that I could replace you." We had a long talk after this with the boss and I was able to keep my precious assignment. I found the silver lining to the black cloud. If the teacher had not come to visit my classroom, we never would have had the opportunity to communicate.

In The Classroom

In the classroom, I have experienced difficult times. However, it is my choice whether to focus upon the black clouds or look for the silver linings. As a teacher, it is my duty to help students to find hope during the dark times in their own lives. For example, if a student fails a test, can I help him or her to find something optimistic about this situation.

On a Personal Note...

I cannot get too caught up in the painful emotions, but must grant myself permission to experience them and look to the future. There will be peaks and valleys, and I must always remember this.

Action for the Day

✓   Today, remember a painful experience with a silver lining.

6 Seconds Moment

◆   Take six seconds to ask yourself what your first reaction is to emotional pain. Should you work to change this response?

#98.
Unruly Kids

"A cross-eyed teacher can keep twice the number of children in order than any other, because the pupils do not know who she's looking at."
John R. Kemble

Concept for Today

Teachers will always have unruly kids in their classrooms. Some teachers may even describe these kids as rotten. There are no rotten kids, only rotten behavior. It is our job to see the potential in all of our students. There are always substantive reasons for kids to act out. Try to see the whole picture when looking at unruly behavior. Teachers need to remember to check their emotions regularly because kids have keen senses and will feed off of a teacher who is angry, frustrated, or irritated. The calmer the teachers can be the better.

In The Classroom

In the classroom, observe and document difficult behaviors. Meet with students one-on-one, and clarify expectations by writing a behavior contract. Always remember that you are here to help students succeed. Be loving, but firm and consistent.

On a Personal Note…

For myself, I recall being an unruly teenager. I caused a great deal of pain for my family by cutting school, being defiant, and running wild. I have worked hard to make amends for my behavior. As a result of my unruly conduct, I have been able to lead my daughter into a different direction and personally connect with my students who have behavior issues.

Action for the Day

- ✓ Today, check your own moods. Remember to remain tranquil and speak calmly. Don't allow any student to provoke you into altering your emotions. Write down your behavior management system and evaluate it. Are you teaching emotional intelligence skills as consequences for inappropriate behaviors?

6 Seconds Moment

- ◆ Take six seconds to check your own feelings and evaluate whether students could feed off of your negative mood today.

#99.
Present Time

"You must live in the present, launch yourself on every wave, and find your eternity in each moment. Fools stand on their island opportunities and look toward another land. There is no other land; there is no other life but this."
Henry David Thoreau

Concept for Today

How many times are we thinking about the past or worrying about the future? Do you ever dream about your job? I know that my mental health is in poor shape when I dream about work. What are the first thoughts that you have each day? When are people truly peaceful and living in the moment? The answer is not often enough. If human beings lived in the present moment a great deal of anxiety would be lifted. Make up your mind to try being in the moment for just one day. If past or present concerns arise, say, "Cancel, cancel, and cancel." Let go of the thought that is interrupting your serenity. To get yourself into the present moment try ringing a bell and taking a deep breath. Place all of your focus, internal and external, upon the present time.

In The Classroom

It is significant to be focused on the here and now, the students, and the task at hand. Students want to have your full attention and many kids act out if they do not receive it. Get into the moment and stay there.

On a Personal Note…

I work to enjoy each and every moment. A practice that helps me is to visit senior centers and the terminally ill. The gift I receive is gaining a deeper appreciation for my own life. I ask myself if I would appreciate each moment more if I knew I had only one month to live.

Action for the Day

- ✓ Today, start to acquire your new habit of living in the present moment. Cancel all negative thoughts and appreciate the here and now.

6 Seconds Moment

- ◆ Take six seconds to remind yourself to stay in the present moment.

#100.
Smile!

"When I smile, not only do I feel happy, but also I bring a ray of light into the lives of others."
Anonymous

Concept for Today

Everyone loves a smile. How often do you smile? Do you walk through life with a smile or frown? Smiling tickles the soul and adds joy to our lives. Try smiling more often and evaluate how you feel. How is a smile from another beneficial?

In The Classroom

In the classroom, students appreciate and will be much more responsive to a teacher who smiles. I am committed to beginning each day by greeting students at the door with a hand shake and smile. It sets a warm and positive classroom tone. Open your heart and extend a smile.

On a Personal Note...

I realized that I did smile a great deal at work, but at home I tended to lose my smile due to being tired and cranky. This changed for me after I recognized that there is delight in seeing family members smile. It gave me great pleasure to see my husband and daughter smile and to know that I am not transferring any black cloud baggage. Now, I try to offer a smile even if I am not at my best. There is a lot more power in a genuine smile.

Action for the Day

✓   Today, smile more often. Acknowledge how a smile makes you feel. Practice saying "Hi" and smiling to as many people as possible. Write down how often you smile throughout the day, how a real smile makes you feel, and the responses that you receive.

6 Seconds Moment

◆   Take six seconds to smile and say "Hello" to someone.

#101.
Dress To Succeed

"Looking good and dressing well is a necessity."
Oscar Wilde

Concept for Today

Mornings have always been tough for me. It takes a little while to remove the cobwebs from my head. To lift my spirits, it helps to dress for success. Dressing appropriately shows the world that I care for myself and am confident.

The youth of today have their own styles. What one wears expresses personal style and individuality. Many of my high school male students often come to school with sagging pants, wearing gang colors, and inappropriate t-shirts. The girls sometimes dress very provocatively. In my classroom we established a rule that boys tuck in their shirts and girls eliminate the low cut blouses. We discuss how dressing appropriately sends messages to all those with whom we interact.

In The Classroom

It is valuable to teach a unit on current fashion or even various historical fashion trends. Kids will gain a perspective on how fashion is shifted by the winds of time.

On a Personal Note…

For myself, I need to think of ways to alter my wardrobe with simple things such as a scarf, hat, or a piece of costume jewelry.

Action for the Day

- ✓ Today, look in your wardrobe and choose a favorite outfit. How do you feel when you wear these clothes? Do you stand a little taller?

6 Seconds Moment

- ◆ Take six seconds to check yourself in the mirror and recognize how professional you look.

#102.
Honor

"Rather fail with honor than succeed by fraud."
Socrates

Concept for Today

What does the word honor mean to you? How do you show yourself honor? Do you ever take a day to honor yourself? What are your values? Is honor one of them? If you witnessed an injustice would you take a stand and speak your mind, even if it meant placing yourself in jeopardy?

In The Classroom

In the classroom, it is valuable to honor your students, so they recognize how much you appreciate them. An extremely powerful activity is creating blue ribbons which say, "I honor you." Beforehand, make ribbons for each student, and then present them, and explain why you are honoring them. Make each reason personal and individual. Also explain that they have one week to pass out blue ribbons to people in their families and community. Tell students that when they honor someone, they must tell them why and also explain that the recipient must continue to pass out blue ribbons to keep the "honor chain" circulating. Have a classroom discussion about their experiences.

On a Personal Note…

For myself, sometimes I lack self-honor because I am often afraid to speak up. However, I recognize that I do not want to live in fear, and that truth is a reigning force in life. Therefore, I may have to plan what I am going to say, and I do try to speak up if I witness an injustice. Honor is one key to happiness, and if I can act as a role model and teach my students and family the value of honor, I am a success.

Action for the Day

- ✓ Today, write down in what ways you have been honorable. Plan a day to honor yourself. Remind yourself that you are a worthy human being who deserves honor in all areas of life.

6 Seconds Moment

- ◆ Take six seconds to think of someone that you will honor with a "blue ribbon."

#103.
Take Out The Paper And The Trash On Thursdays

"We must embrace pain and burn it as fuel for our journey."
Kenji Miyaza

Concept for Today

I was worn out by feelings of day-to-day frustration, worry, and anxiety. I decided to get rid of the trash in my life. I took a period of time to write down my troubles, past and present. I then told myself that I was willing to dump all of the garbage in my life. I took my paper and burned it. I told myself that I was willing to let go of all of the negativity and allow myself to build a positive future.

In The Classroom

In the classroom, I understand that kids come to school with enormous difficulties. Periodically, I ask students to release their troubles on paper and then be ready to move forward with their school day.

On a Personal Note...

For myself, I not only practice the ritual of writing down and burning the negativity in my life, but also practice writing down problems and putting the paper in my, "I'll worry about that tomorrow box." When the trouble has been resolved, I write a little thank you note to whomever.

Action for the Day

- ✓ Today, write down your troubles. Identify a personal practice for releasing them.

6 Seconds Moment

- ◆ Take six seconds to write down one problem. Create plans for removing this challenge in a ritualistic manner. Create a step-by-step plan for removing this challenge.

#104.
Music

"Take a music bath once or twice a week for a few seasons. You will find it is to the soul what a water bath is to the body."
Oliver Wendell Holmes

Concept for Today

Beautiful music is uplifting and touches our souls. I can be very cranky and then an inspiring song changes my mood for the better. Think about the type of music that you enjoy and how it makes you feel. What does an upbeat tune bring up for you? What about a love song or soul music? What are your favorite songs and what is your preferred genre for music? What effect did music have on you as a child? Do you ever hear an "old" song and remember a specific time in your life? Do you enjoy going to concerts? Music is a very powerful healer. Open up your heart and let the music in. Fill your life with beautiful melodies.

In The Classroom

I play music before class begins just to get my mood adjusted and balanced. I then use music as a teaching tool. One of my favorite vocabulary lessons is using "rap" to help students remember words and definitions. They become very engaged and it amazes me how much students remember. Go online and look for lessons that use music. A powerful lesson is to have kids read lyrics to a famous song, and then write about them. Play the song after they are finished writing and discuss which is more powerful, the lyrics or the tune.

On a Personal Note...

For myself, I have truly enjoyed writing this book. However, it was challenging to persevere. At times, I would be tired and there would be no creative energy. Then I would put on a favorite CD and this would inspire me to write.

Action for the Day

✓ Today, write about the music of your youth. Write down your favorite songs. Ask yourself how music makes you feel and observe when it touches your heart.

6 Seconds Moment

◆ Take six seconds to set a date to play a favorite CD, one you have not heard for some time.

#105.
Love

"As you continue to send out love, the energy returns to you in a regenerating spiral. As love accumulates, it keeps your system in balance and harmony. Love is the tool, and more love is the end product."
Sara Paddison

Concept for Today

Love is a key to our wholeness, well-being, joy, and completion. Love is our foundation and our essence. Love helps us to be festive participants in the world.

In The Classroom

I can state that I am truly in love with my job. I may not always feel lovable or loving, but a hunk of my being is love for the teaching profession. My goal as a teacher is to help students fall in love with education and to become "life-long learners." One lesson that my students especially enjoy is my "Jack Canfield's Chicken Soup for the Soul" reading activity. Each of us reads one selection from the book. We then share the stories. I ask each of them to pick a different story to which they write a response. Inevitably a sense of love and compassion unfolds in my classroom as a result of this activity.

On a Personal Note…

For myself, one area of my life that needs improvement is loving myself unconditionally. I have to affirm regularly that I will love myself no matter what my adversities. In addition, I need to lovingly forgive myself when I make a mistake.

Action for the Day

- ✓ Today, choose to come from a state of love rather than fear or anger. Open up your heart and let the love flow in and out. Write down the things that you love about yourself as well as teaching.

6 Seconds Moment

- ◆ Take six seconds to tell yourself that you are lovable and possess a tender heart.

#106.
Apple Trees

"... every tree near our house had a name of its own and special identity. This was the beginning of my love for natural things."
Ellen Glasgow

Concept for Today

Apple trees offer so much with their delicious fruit, shade, and beauty. I can remember my mom having an apple tree in the backyard which she named Elberta. I watched her nurture and care for the tree as if it were a baby. When the fruit ripened, our family enjoyed delicious apple butter, apple sauce, and pies.

I think about a tree and recognize that it starts off as a tiny seed, which, if cared for properly, grows into a fabulous tree. I am reminded that my students are like little seedlings, and if they are loved and nurtured and protected, they too will grow up to be productive adults with many gifts to offer.

In The Classroom

In the classroom, there are so many wonderful activities related to trees. My goal is to help students to grow and realize their gifts. A wonderful activity is to have kids draw a tree. Then partner the kids and have them turn their backs to one another. Each partner takes a turn describing his/her tree and the other person draws it. Many thoughts are generated. We can ask questions such as how clear and detailed were your descriptions? Or, did you add your own ideas without being instructed?

On a Personal Note…

I, too, am like an apple tree. I have grown up to be strong with many fruits or gifts to offer the world. Sometimes I forget this. If you were to imagine yourself as a tree, what would it look like?

Action for the Day

- ✓ Today, draw the image of a beautiful tree. Write words on the trunk that describe you. Write your unique gifts on the branches. Remember to nurture yourself by giving your mind, spirit, and body what they need to continue growing.

6 Seconds Moment

- ◆ Take six seconds to look at a beautiful tree. Enjoy its strength, its beauty, and its contribution to clean air.

#107.
Bright Light

"Light gives of itself freely, filling all available space. It does not seek anything in return; it asks not whether you are friend or foe. It gives of itself and is not thereby diminished."
Michael Strassfeld

Concept for Today

What is the bright light in your life? What makes your heart sing? Is your bright light your family or teaching? What brings brightness to your life? Do you allow yourself to shine your bright light wherever you go? Have you ever experienced darkness and come to realize that there is a light at the end of the tunnel?

In The Classroom

In the classroom, I know that all my students can be bright, shining lights. My goal is to help students keep their lights burning, and in some cases, help students to discover their internal lights. Allow the light into your classroom, by acknowledging kids and helping them to realize that they are unique.

On a Personal Note…

For myself, I have to remember that I am a bright light shining in a world that can be dark. I choose not to stay in the dark by thinking positively and grabbing onto one little ray of light in the form of gratitude.

Action for the Day

✓ Today, remind yourself to look for the bright lights in your life. Ask yourself if you bring light to life's crises. Ask yourself if your light is burning low and needs refueling. How can you accomplish this?

6 Seconds Moment

◆ Take six seconds to think about how you might help your students discover their bright lights.

#108.
Cuts And Bruises

"Pain and suffering are always inevitable for a large intelligence and a deep heart."
Fyodor Dostoyevsky

Concept for Today

Everyone has cuts and bruises from their past. It may be a painful "aha" moment, a time of turmoil, or a loss of someone special. Staying stuck in the past and reliving the pain generates despair and bitterness. Hurts usually have taught us great lessons, such as compassion, perseverance, and how to be courageous in the face of fear.

In The Classroom

I believe that experiencing my own pain and suffering makes me empathetic to students. One thing that helped me to heal was having a trusted friend on whom to lean. As a teacher, I may hear painful life experiences from students. It is my privilege to be their advocate and help them as much as possible.

A subject that sometimes surfaces in my high school class is suicide. When this occurs, I share a story of how I had lost a friend who jumped off the Golden Gate Bridge. My goal is to provide students with information and resources. I also discuss coping mechanisms.

On a Personal Note...

I have experienced that most people do not want to die, but yearn for the hurt and pain to stop. I have come to understand that all pain, cuts, and bruises will heal. Nothing stays the same. I know now that I have coping skills to help with the painful events in life. I also try not to borrow trouble by playing the self-pity game.

Action for the Day

- ✓ Today, write down past cuts and bruises. Then evaluate how you feel about them today.

6 Seconds Moment

- ◆ Take six seconds to identify one way you grew emotionally from an old cut or bruise.

#109.
Think Like A King Or Queen

"Think like a queen. A queen is not afraid to fail. Failure is another stepping stone to greatness."
Oprah Winfrey

Concept for Today

Assume the mantle of a king or queen. Do you feel majestic, confident, poised, and regal? How often do you have days that are filled with self-assuredness and empowerment?

In The Classroom

It can be enlightening to teach about kings, queens, knights, barons, etc. Take this concept and have fun with it. Let your students take turns being king or queen of the classroom. Ask them if they would rule with fairness, kindness, and gentleness or selfishness, tyranny, and greed.

Young children always enjoy stories about princes, kings, and queens. Many little girls pretend to be princesses. One of the happiest stories that I have ever read was "The Paper Bag Princess" by Robert Munsch. This heroic story takes a twist and has Princess Elizabeth rescuing Prince Ronald, then leaving him due to the way he has treated her. (After rescuing the prince from the dragon he has the nerve to negatively comment on her paper bag attire). This heroic story shows us an example of a princess displaying characteristics of a strong, independent female. How do you show your kingly or queenly characteristics?

On a Personal Note...

For myself, like the old TV show, "Queen for a Day," I treat myself royally and with dignity, and occasionally celebrate with a day filled with magnificent treatment, pampering, and relaxation.

Action for the Day

- ✓ Today, write down what your classroom and school would look like if you were the king or queen. Would your subjects be happy?

6 Seconds Moment

- ◆ Take six seconds to think of a royal treat for yourself.

#110.
Memories

"Memory is a way of holding on to the things you love, the things you are, and the things you never want to lose."
Kevin Arnold

Concept for Today

Each person has happy memories. What are your precious memories? Do certain songs bring back special reminiscences? How about looking at pictures? Joyous memories are treasures to be reviewed and shared.

In The Classroom

In the classroom, memories can bring laughter. It is great to have kids make memory books. I have had wonderful outcomes when asking parents to send photos of happy memories in their children's lives. We then take the photos and create collages, along with writing pieces. For older children, we take photos and scan them into computerized Powerpoint presentations or we make mini-movies. While on vacation, students can journal and take pictures. At the end of the school year, they can create memory books and have their classmates autograph them. Encourage your students to create a time capsule with gifts, pictures, newspaper clippings, and letters to be opened on their 30th birthday.

On a Personal Note...

I review happy memories when I need an encouraging moment. Another powerful activity is to reflect upon my own experience in the classroom. Then I use these memories to guide my own teaching methods.

Action for the Day

- ✓ Today, remember who you really are. Keep in mind that you are a beautiful and vibrant teacher filled with experiences and memories which shape the unique person you are today.

6 Seconds Moment

- ◆ Take six seconds to recall a special memory in your life.

#111.
Children: Our Future

"If we are to teach real peace in this world, and if we are to carry on a real war against war, we shall have to begin with the children."
Mohandas Ghandi

Concept for Today

The children of today are the leaders of tomorrow. We need to provide the best education possible, and, in our curriculums, we must help students to develop compassion, thoughtfulness, positive leadership skills, and awareness. If all educators could just do a little each day to help students to believe in themselves and humanity, to develop tolerance and love, then peace and respect could begin to reign.

In The Classroom

We are beginning to make a change. In many schools today, there is a policy called, "Zero Tolerance." This policy is looking out for the well-being and safety of our students. Teachers are intelligent and creative human beings who can overcome obstacles. Let's put our heads together and find ways to influence our kids to be the best.

On a Personal Note...

For myself, I am on the other side of the teaching fence. My students have often committed selfish and horrendous crimes, and need all of the help and guidance that I can give. Between me, the administration, probation, and community outreach programs, we are slowly changing the students' attitudes and behaviors.

I remember one of the happiest moments in my teaching career. I was at the mall when I heard my name being called by one of my former students from Juvenile Hall. He informed me that he was off probation, and going to college. He thanked me for always believing in him and my constant encouragement.

Action for the Day

✓ Today, ask yourself how we can help the children of the world to be their best. What can we do as a society to stop the hate and violence that is occurring in the world? What can you do in your classroom?

6 Seconds Moment

◆ Take six seconds to make a date to find a positive community outreach program to work with your kids.

#112.
Bedtime Routine

"A ruffled mind makes a restless pillow."
Charlotte Brontë

Concept for Today

We all feel refreshed and rejuvenated when we get a good night's sleep. What can you do to ensure that you will get the rest you need? You can take a bubble bath, read a good book, and drink some warm milk mixed with honey and a banana. You can set up a routine that works for you.

In The Classroom

In the classroom, regarding my students, I often wonder about their bedtime routines. To get a glimpse of a student's home life, it is important to get to know the parents. If a student consistently appears tired, an inquiring phone call home can be helpful. Also, establish a trusting relationship with the student and ask them what time they go to bed and if there is anything that is keeping them awake at night.

Teaching students about the value of getting plenty of rest is important. Students need to understand the need to take care of their bodies each and every day. Research is showing that lack of sleep contributes to major health problems such as diabetes.

On a Personal Note…

For myself, I have lived in my body for forty-six years. I know from many late nights that I am not at my best if I do not get eight hours of sleep. When I am over tired, my good judgment and thinking are compromised. When I am over tired, I am also much more sensitive to others' comments; in addition, my responses are less thoughtful.

Action for the Day

- ✓ Today, evaluate your bedtime routine. How many hours of sleep do you require to be at your best? What happens when you are exhausted the next day? Do you release your worries and concerns before you go to sleep?

6 Seconds Moment

- ♦ Take six seconds to make a promise to yourself to get enough rest.

#113.
Your House

"He is the happiest, be he king or peasant, who finds peace in his home."
Johann Wolfgang von Goethe

Concept for Today

Do you ever think about how lucky you are to have a roof over your head? When I am troubled, and feel as if the world is collapsing around me, I have forgotten to be grateful, and have taken for granted such things as my home. It is a powerful nurturing experience to remember to be appreciative for your living space. Do you keep plants or flowers in your home? Is there a fireplace? Do you have a yard? Are there pictures of loved ones placed around the room? Do you have comfortable furniture and cozy blankets? Do you have a quiet space that is your very own? Ask yourself how to make your house a more inviting place of refuge when the world becomes too harsh.

In The Classroom

When I was working with severely autistic children, I had the honor of doing home visits. It gave me a powerful peek at what was going on outside of school. An intriguing lesson plan is having students draw floor plans of their homes. If a justification is needed, have kids draw an emergency escape plan.

We must remember that our classrooms are students' second homes. Sometimes, I walk into my classroom and ask myself if I like it here, as it is a place where I spend so much time. Have your students ask this question as well. If the answer is "no," what changes could be made?

On a Personal Note...

There is no place like home. I am truly grateful for this but also know that many people are less fortunate. I try to remember the homeless by serving hot meals at the local shelter or buying the ingredients for a family's Thanksgiving meal and providing a check for the turkey.

Action for the Day

- ✓ Today, think about your home and describe it. Ask yourself what feelings you get when you enter the doorway. Does your home offer rejuvenation, peace, and contentment? Do you consider your classroom a place that feels like home?

6 Seconds Moment

- ◆ Take six seconds to think of your favorite place in your classroom. Take another six seconds to contemplate creating a second favorite spot.

#114.
Enthusiasm

"Get excited and enthusiastic about your own dream. This excitement is like a forest fire— you can smell it, taste it, and see it from a mile away."
Denis Waitley

Concept for Today

Do you ever look back and recall how enthusiastic and excited you were about your first teaching job? Do you still enjoy this same level of involvement in your current job? If not, how many days out of the year are you truly enthusiastic? Five days, or one hundred and five days?

In The Classroom

In the classroom, I confess I am not always Mrs. Sunshine bursting with enthusiasm. I know that I have to work at it. I accomplish this by re-evaluating lesson plans and making sure that there is at least one weekly lesson or topic that I am especially passionate about and that emotionally impacts my students. I remember one of the reasons that I went into teaching in the first place was to help students fall in love with learning. If one lesson can motivate them, I am a success. To recharge my passion for teaching, I can collaborate with another teacher and work on creating a dynamite lesson which will not only touch my heart but my students' hearts as well.

On a Personal Note…

Life, problems, and obstacles have a tendency to decrease my day-to-day eagerness. To reignite my enthusiasm, I grab onto one lesson, one student, or one incident for focus. It acts like a yellow highlight in my brain.

Action for the Day

- ✓ Today, make a list of events in your personal life about which you are enthusiastic. Identify why. How many of these can you share with your students?

6 Seconds Moment

- ◆ Take six seconds to make a conscious decision to meet with a trusted and enthusiastic teacher to share ideas about lesson plans and teaching.

#115.
Twelve Hugs A Day

"We need 4 hugs a day for survival. We need 8 hugs a day for maintenance. We need 12 hugs a day for growth."
Virginia Satir

Concept for Today

There is so much power and healing in the human touch. We seek massages, perform body work, and, if we are hurt, we automatically touch the painful area. Touch is an innate ability of all human beings. Do you get twelve hugs a day? Or are you the type of person who does not care to be touched? Human beings thrive from another person's touch. So open your heart and allow yourself to experience more embraces, hugs, pats on the back, and hand holding. If you see an old friend, what is your physical reaction? Remember, our souls thrive on physical contact. Give twelve hugs a day.

In The Classroom

When I worked with students who suffered from the condition of autism, one of their biggest issues was touch and sensory overload. For an autistic child, a hug or pat on the back can be a painful experience. As a teacher, I have always respected proximity and spatial boundaries with students. After working many years with one autistic boy, a trusting relationship has been established and he is able to give me a high five and a smile each time he sees me.

On a Personal Note…

For myself, if the situation calls for it, I enjoy giving friends, co-workers, and family great big hugs. This has not always been the case, due to the fact that my father did not have the ability for showing affection. Looking back, I realize that this was a great loss for both of us.

Action for the Day

- ✓ Today, ask yourself what you think of hugs between colleagues. Are you a warm person who gives hugs? Do you get enough physical contact each day?

6 Seconds Moment

- ◆ Take six seconds to give a colleague a great, big hug.

#116.
Change

"Only I can change my life. No one can do it for me."
Carol Burnett

Concept for Today

People always say that change is good for a person even though it may be uncomfortable. Change helps us to grow as human beings. Do you ever think about making a change in your life? Do you ever ask yourself what your life might look like if you made some drastic changes? What would they be? It may be difficult to make a change even when you know in your heart it will help you. What prevents people from making changes? Can you identify six reasons for not making tough changes you have been promising yourself, in areas such as diet, smoking, exercise, or social contact, etc?

In The Classroom

In the classroom, change is often a positive shift. I remember a drastic change that had to be made several years ago. Since I was a special education teacher working with kids who had behavior disorders, I had allowed each student thirty minutes of free internet time as an incentive. Students took advantage of the situation and went to sites that were entertainment only and not education-oriented. I notified students that there would no longer be any free internet time. Of course, the students grumbled and complained, but grew accustomed to the new dictate. I helped them understand that this change was beneficial.

On a Personal Note...

I always want to change my life by slowing down, strengthening my humanitarianism, and really appreciating life on a daily basis.

Action for the Day

- ✓ Today, think about how you deal with change in your life. Do you embrace change, or do you despise it? How do you handle extreme changes in your life such as an unexpected death, financial difficulties, or a necessary career move? In your classroom, do you make changes to improve your teaching? Do you change your lesson plans based on the moment?

6 Seconds Moment

- ◆ Take six seconds to affirm that change may be a positive thing, even if it takes you out of your comfort zone.

#117.
Shoes

"Arithmetic is being able to count up to twenty without taking off your shoes."
Mickey Mouse

Concept for Today

Every day we get up and get ready for the day. We dress, slip on our shoes, and begin our day's path. Where will your shoes take you? Will they take you on a positive daily path or a negative one? Will your shoes hurt your feet and cause discomfort throughout your day? Shoes can offer us protection, comfort, and complete our attire. Fashionable shoes may help you feel good about your self-image. Shoes that look good, but hurt your feet are worthless. Many people have a huge selection of shoes. What do your shoes say about you? Where will your shoes take you today?

In The Classroom

In the classroom, I present a creative writing activity called, "The Shoe Escapade." Students are required to write a story about an adventure that a pair of shoes might have. They are to take the point of view of the shoes. Students respond to questions such as what do the shoes look like, where do they travel, how far do they go, what obstacles do they encounter, do they meet any other pairs of shoes along the way, and what happens when they meet one shoe that has lost its partner.

On a Personal Note…

For myself, I consider my shoes to be a vehicle for my life's path. My hope for each day is to create a path filled with hope, optimism, philanthropy, and self-respect. At the end of the day, before going to sleep, I like to reflect upon my day and evaluate how it went. Where did my shoes take me today?

Action for the Day

- ✓ Today, think about your life's journey. Write down what your journey looks like. Where are you on the road of life?

6 Seconds Moment

- ◆ Take six seconds to look at the shoes you are wearing today and ask yourself what they say about you.

#118.
Inventory

"A careful inventory of all your past experiences may disclose the startling fact that everything has happened for the best."
Anonymous

Concept for Today

How often do you take inventory of your classroom supplies, items in your home, and your life? Taking inventory of your materials and possessions is a positive, uplifting experience. Purging unnecessary items makes room for better things to come your way. Unfortunately, many people get caught up in the daily routines of life and forget to take stock and let go of what no longer suits them. Are you a person who holds on to things no matter how obsolete or old? More importantly, do you ever take the time to inventory your life and work on making positive changes?

In The Classroom

I once realized that I had neglected to inventory my teaching materials. Of course, I always had my favorite books and lessons, but what were these other bits? I had held onto things that I never use. I was amazed at how many times I have walked past my bookshelf and never paid attention to what is on it or to the hundreds of unused files in my cabinet. I asked myself why I was hanging onto so much clutter. Since time is always a factor and I am an extremely busy teacher, I decided to inventory one shelf at a time. I told myself that just for today, I could clean and get rid of books on one shelf. This method was very helpful and it was amazing to discover the books that had outlived their usefulness.

On a Personal Note…

For myself, I also decided to take inventory of behaviors that no longer helped me. I sat down and wrote a list of habits and behaviors that were unhealthy. After doing this ritual, I tore up the paper and let it go. Then to ensure that I was making progress, I initiated a mini-inventory ritual before bed. I asked myself if I had exhibited any behaviors throughout the day that I was trying to eliminate.

Action for the Day

- ✓ Today, set aside some time to inventory your life. List the habits, behaviors, and personality characteristics that no longer serve your highest good.

6 Seconds Moment

- ◆ Take six seconds to pick an area in your home or classroom that needs to be inventoried and organized. Then decide when you can tackle the job.

#119.
Resentment

"Holding on to anger, resentment and hurt only gives you tense muscles, a headache and a sore jaw from clenching your teeth. Forgiveness gives you back the laughter and the lightness in your life."
Joan Lunden

Concept for Today

For so many years, I held on to unresolved resentments toward people who had caused me harm. I became aware of resentments when an innocent someone would irritate me and I would escalate quickly to anger. Resentment is an ugly emotion that is a curtain for antagonism, anger, and rage. At work, if a co-worker or boss angered me, I would suppress the emotion. After all, I was a professional and could not vent my anger at work. As a result, my anger and resentment would escalate in front of my family.

I identified that I had unresolved resentments and needed to search for ways to forgive. I began the process by making a list of people who needed my forgiveness. I was amazed that I had resentments that were thirty years old. There was something magical about writing these names down on paper. Other times I simply made a conscious decision to forgive.

In The Classroom

It is a powerful analysis to recognize if you are easily angered by any one student. Ask yourself how you would like a teacher to handle the situation if you were the student. What do you learn from this activity? Grant yourself permission to work on resentments and know that they are a part of human nature. However, there are steps we can take to grow and release negativity.

On a Personal Note…

For myself, angry resentment has taken a nasty bite out of my soul in the past. Every time I relive the past hurt and fixate on the wrong that has occurred, I continue to drown in emotional pain. By practicing the art of forgiveness I am set free from resentment and cranky moods.

Action for the Day

- ✓ Today, identify what your bad moods look like and identify how often you have them. Do you think you are harboring resentments?

6 Seconds Moment

- ◆ Take six seconds to forgive someone toward whom you are resentful. Take another six seconds to wish them the best.

#120.
Always Hold On Tight To Your Dreams

"Dream what you want to dream; go where you want to go; be what you want to be, because you have only one life and one chance to do all the things you want to do."
Anonymous

Concept for Today

When we are young, we often hear people tell us to dream, and never let go of our dreams. Wouldn't it be nice if everyone held onto their dreams and pursued them? Have you lost your dreams and given up? What happens to our childhood dreams?

In The Classroom

In the classroom, always encourage your students to dream. Teach them that their dreams can come true. If you feel comfortable, share some of your dreams with your students. Offer encouragement and provide steps for accomplishing dreams so your students will move forward. Teach a unit on pursuing dreams. Show vignettes from the film with Will Smith called "The Pursuit of Happyness." Share stories of unlikely heroes who have made their dreams come true.

On a Personal Note…

For myself, when things became dark and depressing, I stopped dreaming. However, throughout my darkness, I still had my tiny, inner voice reminding me that I had dreamed of having a college education. I began to share my dream with others, who encouraged me, and then I made a plan to pursue it. When I received my first undergraduate report card, I realized that this was a gigantic step forward.

Action for the Day

- ✓ Today, identify your dreams. Write them down. Remind yourself that action can make dreams come true, even if you have lost dreams in the past.

6 Seconds Moment

- ♦ Take six seconds to capture one of your dreams. Set a time to design a plan for dream fulfillment.

#121.
Insane Behavior

"Insanity is often the logic of an accurate mind over tasked."
Oliver Wendell Holmes, Sr.

Concept for Today

Albert Einstein presented a definition of the word insanity which has stuck with me throughout the years. He said that insanity really means repeating the same behavior and expecting different results. I had to ask myself how often I commit insane behaviors. The answer is, often. Some days, I just feel engulfed in insanity. My own definition of insanity is chaos in all areas of my life, plus a desperate feeling of being overwhelmed. When I feel this way, it leads to erratic emotions, tears, and powerlessness. Self-assessment helps me evaluate my behaviors and look for alternatives.

In The Classroom

In the classroom, there are many days when I feel that "insanity" is swallowing me up. My students are at different academic levels, some students do not speak English, some have behavior problems, and standardized tests are coming up. At this point, I go back to basics and do what I can for this day. The question remains, "How can I help each student progress and achieve?" I then take small, but consistent steps to help the kids move forward.

On a Personal Note…

For myself, I realize that I am extra sensitive. I like my sensitivity when it comes to the art of teaching, but can do without it when it comes to magnifying trouble. At this point, I might do something physical, such as walking. The longer that I walk the more the insanity fades.

Action for the Day

- ✓ Today, if you feel overwhelmed or that insanity is taking over, make a game plan. Write down what you can do to help yourself when life comes tumbling down around you.

6 Seconds Moment

- ◆ Take six seconds for a deep breath. Remind yourself not to take overwhelming feelings too seriously.

#122.
Depression

"Noble deeds and hot baths are the best cures for depression."
Dodie Smith

Concept for Today

Nearly everyone suffers from some degree of depression. Depression can be caused by a chemical imbalance, a painful life situation, or an abundance of life traumas. What are your mechanisms for handling the "blues"? How long do the sad feelings last? I learned a tough life lesson regarding depression. I discovered that there are hurt feelings caused by the episode itself and then there are different, painful feelings which show that I am healing.

I do not like to hurt or feel sad. I would stuff my feelings, push them inside or brush them under the carpet. However, I came to realize that I honor myself by feeling my pain, identifying the emotions, then allowing grieving and healing time.

In The Classroom

In the classroom, I always observe and check in to see how students are feeling. I like to start the day by asking students to rate how they are feeling between a one and a ten, (i.e., one being the least and ten being the best). If one of my students seems to be continuously down, I talk to him/her, and also alert my school psychologist or principal. I really do not want my students suffering. I also like to teach my students lessons about optimism, perseverance, and hope.

On a Personal Note...

For myself, I have experienced both long and short-term depression. Medication has been utilized, as well as creating a list of techniques to help. Helping another person in need has been a wonderful antidote for my depression.

Action for the Day

- ✓ Today, evaluate how often you get depressed and to what degree. Write down coping methods for when you experience depression.

6 Seconds Moment

- ♦ Take six seconds to remember the last time you were depressed or feeling "blue". How did you recover?

#123.
Dry Boring Content

"A speaker who does not strike oil in ten minutes should stop boring his audience."
Anonymous

Concept for Today

As human beings there are some areas of our lives that are dry and boring. At work, do you ever find yourself looking at the clock and wishing time would pass? How can we add some "spice" to our hum-drum lives? How can we add some "puppy dog tails"?

In The Classroom

Kids also get bored and turned off to school. It is my job to take some time and energy to think outside of the box when creating lessons and units. For example, here are two California state standards: 3.0 Students move beyond a particular problem by generalizing to other situations: 3.2 Note the method of deriving the solution and demonstrate a conceptual understanding of the derivation by solving similar problems. How dry! I look at these two standards and try to think up an interesting way to meet them. One idea is to have students design a poster with the three math problems that they like best from the lesson. On the poster, they must include both visuals and math language, and then present their ideas to their classmates with a gallery walk. I then present a grab bag activity in which I will have similar math problems written on cards and students will "pick" and "solve". Teachers are creative and can find a variety of ways to make the curriculum engaging and intriguing.

On a Personal Note...

There are many times I take a boring task and make a game out of it. For example, when folding my daughter's socks, I list adjectives about her that start with "s".

Action for the Day

- ✓ Today, write down some areas and situations that are tedious. Pick one and think of how you could make that task more interesting.

6 Seconds Moment

- ♦ Take six seconds to plan a change in your daily routine, such as taking an alternate route to work, brushing your teeth with your left hand, contacting a long lost friend from whom you have not heard in ages.

#124.
Troubled Times

"Ultimately, we have just one moral duty: to reclaim large areas of peace in ourselves, more and more peace, and to reflect it towards others. And the more peace there is in us, the more peace there will be in our troubled world."
Etty Hilsum

Concept for Today

History always repeats itself. There are wars, human suffering, starvation, intolerance, diseases, homicide, and hatred. How do we maintain a positive attitude when so many atrocities are occurring in our world? Do we come from a place of constant fear, or a place of hope? How do we keep ourselves feeling safe? Do we commit to making the world a better place? Do we work hard to make decisions that are helpful for our society? Do we strive to teach our children that they can make a difference?

In The Classroom

In the classroom, I believe that teachers are responsible for much more than just teaching academics. We need to prepare our children to handle the world's problems with positive power, strength, and courage. In my classroom, I make small differences each and every day by treating students with respect, teaching students to be collaborative and cooperative with one another, and helping students to develop creative strategies for solving problems. I let kids know that their opinions count.

On a Personal Note…

For myself, to demonstrate that I am making a difference, I volunteer once a month in a senior citizen home. My daughter and I both participate and dress up as clowns who sing the old time songs. It brings us closer, plus makes a difference in the lives of others. We have noted the peaceful feelings we experience on our way home.

Action for the Day

- ✓ Today make a list of five things that you can do throughout the week to add peace to your home, and classroom.

6 Seconds Moment

- ◆ Take six seconds to identify one way you can contribute to the peace the world needs.

#125. Success

"Success is liking yourself, liking what you do, and liking how you do it."
Maya Angelou

Concept for Today

Each person on this planet has had major and minor successes. Believing that you are a successful human being is like breath to the body. Each individual has triumphant life successes and little mini-successes. How do you define success? I like to take the definition of success to a higher level than simply prestige and materialistic gain. For me, it means I have friends, my family trusts me, and colleagues respect my opinion. Where are you with your successes? How many days per week do you feel successful?

In The Classroom

I consider each day a success if I have accomplished a mini-task, such as being friendly to students and co-workers, persevering even with huge obstacles, or simply smiling and appreciating life. To keep the passion of teaching alive, I must acknowledge all successes. By paying homage to my own successes, I am able to help students recognize theirs. To honor my students, no matter what their ages or abilities, I enjoy putting their work up on a bulletin board called the "Wall of Fame".

On a Personal Note…

For myself, if I get up out of bed and face each day, I am a success. By continuously showing up for work, family, and life, I am a success. If I have helped myself and another, it has been a successful day. The beauty of life is that I get a new opportunity to be successful each day.

Action for the Day

- ✓ Today, make a list of both your gigantic successes and your tiny successes in life. Respond to the question, "How can I be successful on a daily basis?"

6 Seconds Moment

- ♦ Take six seconds to identify one reason why you are a successful human being.

#126.
Birthdays

"If there's something that you're dreaming of then may it all come true, because you deserve it all...HAPPY BIRTHDAY."
Anonymous

Concept for Today

Birthdays are the best! The world is a better place because you are here. So many people dread their birthdays and miss out on the opportunity to celebrate their lives, triumphs, gifts, and experiences. People see a number which they may not like and allow pride to get in the way of enjoying their birthdays. Why does society get caught up with age and false pride? Remember how much fun birthdays were when you were a child? Birthdays need to be celebrated. This is a time to really acknowledge who you are and where you are on the road of life. No matter what your age, there are more adventures and good times coming your way. So on your birthday, put on your party hat and celebrate. Rejoice upon how far you have come in life and cherish who you are. It is your special, happy day.

In The Classroom

In the classroom, all students love to have their birthdays celebrated no matter what their ages. I know that most older students' mothers will not be bringing in cupcakes and party hats for the class. So, as a teacher who honors kids, how can you celebrate an older child's birthday? I enjoy decorating their desk and chair, giving a birthday card, and a sparkly, flavored water. My students always appreciate this act of kindness.

On a Personal Note...

After childhood, I hated my birthdays. After the age of twenty-one, they certainly did not seem as important or fun. However, after growing a little wiser, I have come to believe that my birthday is special and needs to be celebrated. I open myself up to friends and family and allow myself to receive other people's gifts and kindnesses.

Action for the Day

- ✓ Today, write down what your birthday means to you and how you usually celebrate it. Write down how you celebrate loved one's birthdays. What is your custom for celebrating student birthdays?

6 Seconds Moment

- ◆ Take six seconds to determine how to add one original ingredient for the next birthday on your list.

#127.
Gifts That Keep On Giving

"A hug is the perfect gift; one size fits all, and nobody minds if you exchange it."
Irvin Ball

Concept for Today

Ask yourself what gifts you give to others. Do you remember to show other people how much you appreciate them? Do you give gifts that will touch people's hearts? Are they better because they have known you? What gifts have you given that will have a positive effect on others and will provide continuous joy? The gifts that keep on giving do not have to have a price tag attached. These gifts can be a smile, a positive comment, a shoulder to lean on, a hug, a phone call, and your love.

In The Classroom

In the classroom, teachers continuously give gifts that will have a life-long effect on students. We open the gate for learning and understanding. We provide the keys to wisdom, we model patience, we give our hearts, we teach children to be resilient, to solve problems and to be deep thinkers. We provide lessons that students will remember, comprehend, and enjoy. Our students will utilize the knowledge which we provide. We help kids to develop a passion for life-long learning.

On a Personal Note…

I ask the question, "Are my students better off for being in my classroom? Have I helped students to enjoy their academic experience? If I have a substitute, will I be missed?" So many times, I have heard students report that they hate school. Have I helped students to change their attitude after being in my classroom?

Action for the Day

✓ Today, be mindful that the gifts that you provide students, co-workers, and family are gifts that keep on giving. Contemplate whether you have been a positive influence on others.

6 Seconds Moment

◆ Take six seconds to think of three gifts that you will give throughout your week.

#128.
Attitude Matters

"You cannot control what happens to you, but you can control your attitude toward what happens to you, and in that, you will be mastering change rather than allowing it to master you."
Brian Tracy

Concept for Today

Our attitudes are critical; they can either make us or break us. A positive attitude can help us to live a rich life filled with joy, wellness, and hope. A negative attitude can fill us with despair, anger, and resentment. What type of attitude have you chosen up to this point?

In The Classroom

In the classroom, teachers will discover many different types of attitudes with students and colleagues. With our peers, who may possess a "not so nice attitude," we can put on our virtual optimism raincoat to avoid absorbing their attitudes. We can then still be as kind as possible, while maintaining our boundaries. With students, when there are poor attitudes, remember that they need encouragement.

On a Personal Note...

I work on maintaining a positive attitude. I know how contagious feelings are and therefore prefer to spread a joyful, uplifting virus rather than a depressing one.

Action for the Day

- ✓ Today, think about your overall attitude. Is it usually positive or negative? When you do possess a negative attitude, what are the results? What can you do to build a positive attitude?

6 Seconds Moment

- ◆ Take six seconds to check your attitude on a scale of one to ten (one being the lowest and ten being the highest). Take another 6 seconds to raise it higher.

#129.
Rolling With The Punches

"Character cannot be developed in ease and quiet. Only through experience of trial and suffering can the soul be strengthened, ambition inspired, and success achieved."
Helen Keller

Concept for Today

Once, instead of teaching my self-contained, special day class, I was notified that I would be teaching single-subject reading for one week. Administration notified me of this on Friday and the new assignment would begin on Monday. (I knew I could roll with the punches). I was also told that I would be team teaching. Of course, I collaborated with the other teacher, and she told me that she would have Monday's lesson prepared.

On Monday I was told fifteen minutes before class that the other teacher was absent. I started scrambling to pull a lesson together for one hundred students with whom I had never worked. Having new kids who would undoubtedly test me and the Monday blues rocked my world. Even though I had over ten years teaching experience, it was like being a new teacher all over again. I knew that providing an interesting lesson would minimize behavior problems. At the end of the day, I was exhausted, but proud. I had rolled with the punches and walked out a winner. I had provided a dynamite lesson. This opportunity gave me the chance to see what I could do under severe pressure.

In The Classroom

By being flexible and open minded, as well as calm, teachers can be ready for anything. This sudden shift in my teaching assignment made me acknowledge my talents, strengths, and abilities that developed over the years. It was a day for celebrating my gifts. Challenges allow us to grow as professionals.

On a Personal Note...

Life often throws me punches. Effectively handling obstacles and unexpected events helps me to grow as a human being.

Action for the Day

- ✓ Write down how you roll with the punches of life. What are your coping skills for change, crisis, and the unexpected?

6 Seconds Moment

- ♦ Take six seconds to stop, clear your mind, and make a commitment to "roll with the punches" today.

#130.
A Recipe For Teaching

"My recipe for life is not being afraid of myself, afraid of what I think or of my opinions."
Eartha Kitt

Concept for Today

What is your favorite recipe? Think about the elements of a great recipe. Do you have a recipe for your life? How about teaching? If you created a recipe for your life, what would it look like? What happens if you follow all of the steps in your recipe but skip an ingredient or bake it for too long? Do you ever find yourself overcooked? What types of ingredients are needed to be a well-rounded, happy human being? What do you need to be delicious on the inside and scrumptious on the outside?

In The Classroom

A great lesson for either math or science is having students work with recipes. Measuring, mixing, and preparing something delicious and nutritious is always fun for kids. A treasured project is to ask students to bring in their favorite recipes for a class cookbook. For all kids, look for unusual and unique holidays, special occasions, or classroom ethnicities in order to incorporate food into any core subject.

On a Personal Note...

For myself, I have constructed my life's recipe. I started off with ingredients such as kindness, love, security, strength, trust, peace, creativity, compassion, and understanding. I then mixed these ingredients together and decided that I needed to bake for an hour and a half until crispy on the outside, (because I need a bit of a protective crust), but still rich and firm on the inside to remind me that my strength comes from my inner self. I then may need to be reheated if I become cold.

Action for the Day

- ✓ Today, write down a recipe that describes your life. Also create a recipe for your teaching style.

6 Seconds Moment

- ◆ Take six seconds to decide what essential ingredients would be a part of your recipe for teaching.

#131.
Gut-Wrenching News

"Instead of weeping when a tragedy occurs in a songbird's life, it sings away its grief. I believe we could well follow the pattern of our feathered friends."
Anonymous

Concept for Today

Each of us will receive devastating news – a death in the family, loss of a job, a serious illness, extreme financial trouble, or another unfortunate event. How do you cope with distressing news? Do you go into a state of shock? Do you feel as if the air has been sucked out of your body? Do you cry? Do you shut down? What is your process?

In The Classroom

There will be times when students will face upsetting news. I can recall that in the first grade one of my best friends died in a bicycle accident. I recall how grief stricken and shocked I was.

During our teaching careers, we may experience the loss of a beloved student. Also, I can recall working with teachers who were diagnosed with cancer. Hopefully we are strong enough to help our students through these tragedies. Thank goodness for guidance and grief counselors. My wish is to always offer support and love during these difficult times.

On a Personal Note...

I have experienced troubling news. One day at work, a favorite co-worker of mine complained of a terrible headache. While teaching English, she suddenly collapsed and the paramedics had to be called. CPR was done but to no avail. Our school staff received the gut-wrenching news that our beloved teacher had passed away from a brain aneurysm. The saddest part was that she had two young daughters who would grow up without a mother.

Action for the Day

- ✓ Today, write down a time when you received gut-wrenching news. How did you handle it? Also contemplate how you will support that child who experiences devastating news.

6 Seconds Moment

- ◆ Take six seconds to rate yourself from one (low) to ten (high) on how strong you think you are emotionally.

#132.
Gentle Whisper

"I think we all have a little voice inside us that will guide us. It may be God, I don't know. But I think that if we shut out all the noise and clutter from our lives and listen to that voice, it will tell us the right thing to do."
Christopher Reeve

Concept for Today

We each have an inner voice. How often do you slow down enough to hear this gentle whisper? Do you recall being a young child and listening to what your parents identified as your conscience? What did your conscience say when you were about to be naughty? As adults bogged down with day-to-day frustrations, deadlines, commitments, worries, and commotion, we forget to listen to our inner voices. Can you center yourself so you can hear your inner voice? Do you listen to this voice when making decisions?

In The Classroom

In the classroom, teachers make hundreds of decisions each day. The questions that we need to ask ourselves include, "Do I listen to my own inner voice or do I act automatically? Am I so busy or so stuck that I make my decisions without thinking?" It is so helpful to slow down and get in touch with the gentle whispers of your inner voice.

On a Personal Note…

For myself, I definitely have a conscience. Sometimes it nags me. However, when I listen to my inner voice or conscience, especially before acting, I receive the gift of peace. Sometimes I help myself to slow down and hear my inner voice by taking a walk, journaling, or doing a brief meditation.

Action for the Day

- ✓ Today, identify a recent decision that you had to make. Was it fear based or guided by the gentleness of your inner voice?

6 Seconds Moment

- ◆ Take six seconds to be absolutely still and quiet, and listen to a suggestion from your inner voice.

#133.
Amends

"Guilt is the very nerve of sorrow."
Horace Bushnell

Concept for Today

Have you ever watched the TV show called, "My Name is Earl" created by Greg Garcia? I love the fact that the show is based upon making amends for wrongs done toward others. If I am wrong, I try to promptly admit it. What do you do when you have said or done something that hurts another person? Do you brush it under the carpet or attempt reconciliation?

If we do things that harm others and do not clean up the mess, we hurt ourselves. Guilt arrives to devour our bodies and spirits. Having a guilty conscience is like wearing dirty under garments. Your outer attire may be sharp and attractive, but on the inside you need a change.

In The Classroom

Students make mistakes on a daily basis. It is part of the learning process. My hope for all teachers is that no one makes the mistake of intensifying guilt. We want our students to know that it is okay to make a mistake and that they will not be humiliated, blamed, or shamed. My number one goal in the classroom is to provide a safe learning environment in which students can express themselves and not worry about being ridiculed or made to feel more guilty. I will not allow shame or blame.

On a Personal Note…

For myself, as a child, I not only had to say I am sorry but was taught to hold onto the remorse. As a result, if I made a mistake, I beat myself up, and would be afraid to make amends.

Action for the Day

- ✓ Today, if you harm another, immediately make a sincere apology and move forward.

6 Seconds Moment

- ♦ Take six seconds to think of a person to whom you owe amends.

#134.
I Have A Date With Myself!

"Plant your own garden and decorate your own soul, instead of waiting for someone to bring you flowers."
Veronica A. Shoffstall

Concept for Today

Make plans to have a fabulous date tonight with yourself. What will you do? How can you make the night perfect for yourself? I often plan for a time when I know I will have the house to myself. On my way home from school I stop at the grocery store and buy a favorite delicacy, some flowers, and a fantastic dessert just for me. After cooking a delicious meal, I enjoy an old-time classic movie. I love having special dates for myself.

In The Classroom

In the classroom, students need to learn how important it is to know themselves. I give self-interest inventories in order to know my students better and to help them grow in self-knowledge, and appreciation. I also have the goal of teaching students that loving and caring for one's self is not a selfish act. We often brainstorm ways to care for ourselves, including exercise, fun reading, spending time with a friend, baking goodies, and sharing the results. I often ask them to share the results in a journal entry.

On a Personal Note...

For myself, if I take good care of "me," I can better care for others. I need to remember this due to the fact that I was reared during a time that it was considered selfish to think of yourself. Not so!

Action for the Day

✓ Today, plan a fabulous date with yourself. What will you do? When will this date take place?

6 Seconds Moment

◆ Take six seconds to make a commitment that you will plan more dates with you and only you. Only one admission ticket will be granted.

#135.
When You Need A Shoulder To Cry On

"The ultimate lesson all of us have to learn is unconditional love, which includes not only others but ourselves as well."
Elisabeth Kübler-Ross

Concept for Today

On the road of life, there will be times when you need a friend to lean upon. Do you have a friend who loves you unconditionally and to whom you can turn when life delivers you lemons? Who is that person? Do you have more than one special friend?

In The Classroom

I enjoy having students do writing samples about the qualities of a true friend. I also ask if they themselves possess these essential qualities. Another lesson that I enjoy teaching is having kids listen to, read, and analyze the lyrics for the popular song, "Lean on Me," by Bill Withers. We then have a grand conversation on the meaning of true friendship.

On a Personal Note…

I do, in fact, have a special friend upon whom I can lean at any time. Perhaps more importantly, I know that I am also a special friend to others. In other words, I want to provide a shoulder to others when it is needed.

Action for the Day

✓ Today, think of a person who loves you unconditionally. What is special about this person? Do you surround yourself with people who truly care about you? Ask yourself if you offer a shoulder for other people to cry upon. Who do you love unconditionally?

6 Seconds Moment

♦ Take six seconds to identify the ingredient required so that your shoulders are strong enough to support yourself and another.

#136.
Surrender

"The greatness of a man's power is the measure of his surrender."
William Booth

Concept for Today

There have been times in my life when I had to surrender and accept the situation. For example, I had to surrender when my mother-in-law lost her fight against ovarian cancer. I had to surrender when a company, that supposedly was helping me manage my credit, cheated me.

Surrendering does not mean weakness of character, but shows courage. Ask for help with huge problems. Think creatively through the situation and, if your multiple attempts do not bring the outcomes desired, then weigh the costs and the benefits of continuing. If costs outweigh the benefits, give yourself permission to throw in the towel.

In The Classroom

Hopefully, there will be very few times requiring surrender. We must remember that we might not be able to help every child in the way that we want. For example, we may have a student who cannot read. We give that child every ounce of encouragement, our wisdom, and employ all the learning mechanisms which should help. For some strange reason, we may not succeed. This is where we have to seek outside help and surrender to the present situation.

On a Personal Note...

For myself, I have had to surrender many times. It may be my greatest asset to know when to surrender. When I surrender over negative situations and utilize that energy in productive ways life becomes a little bit nicer for everyone.

Action for the Day

- ✓ Today, think of a time in your life when you had to surrender either personally or professionally. Did something ultimately help?

6 Seconds Moment

- ◆ Take six seconds to grant yourself permission to surrender when necessary.

#137.
Replenish Yourself

"Reach out your hand if your cup be empty, if your cup is full may it be again."
Robert Hunter

Concept for Today

We are so busy running, doing, and giving that we often forget to replenish ourselves. We pay more attention to keeping our gas tanks filled than refilling our own energy.

Sit quietly for a moment, and ask yourself if you are running on empty, are half full, or perhaps overflowing with energy, enthusiasm, clarity, and positive emotional well-being. If you find yourself empty, or partially depleted, how can you nurture yourself in order to become filled with joy, vigor, passion, and exuberance? What do you need in order to re-charge your batteries? If you find yourself overflowing with positive, physical, and emotional abundance, how can you maintain this state?

In The Classroom

In the classroom, how do you keep your students rejuvenated and refreshed? Do you ever observe students looking bored, uninterested, or falling asleep? What can you do as a creative teacher to keep students engaged? You can have contests, group activities, class projects with social networking, and student-led activities. Put your kids in the driver's seat doing presentations. By providing lessons that are student driven, you will receive the gift of low teacher micro-management.

On a Personal Note...

I know what it is like to experience exhaustion and mental shut-down. I have to remind myself to engage in a mentally stimulating activity unrelated to work. When I feel rejuvenated, I take time to straighten out the imbalances which are occurring in my life.

Action for the Day

- ✓ Today, pick one activity that will kindle your spirit. This could be going to the movies, taking a nap, going out to dinner, or spending time with a treasured friend. If time is an issue, you could do a mini-activity such as deep breathing, watching a favorite TV show, going to bed early, or listening to music. The important thing to remember is that as an educator you must care for yourself before caring for others.

6 Seconds Moment

- ◆ Take six seconds to think of one major and one minor restoration activity.

#138.
Talents And Gifts

"I believe that life is a journey, often difficult and sometimes incredibly cruel, but we are well equipped for it if only we tap into our talents and gifts and allow them to blossom."
Les Brown

Concept for Today

All people have unique gifts and talents. More will be discovered as we venture through life. Can you identify yours? How can you tap into them? Reflecting upon your childhood and recalling things that you loved to do might help you to rediscover them.

In The Classroom

It is my job to help kids discover their strengths and abilities. I do this by observing how engaged a child is in any particular lesson. If a child is enthusiastic about something, I encourage them with all of my heart. One of my students told me that he was going to be a drug dealer when he grew up. I had heard these negative comments, and contemplated how I might fight that point of view. Later that day, I showed a video about Barack Obama's life. I identified many of the wonderful qualities that Barack had and told the student that he also possessed many of the same gifts, such as warmth, charisma, and intelligence. This student half-listened to me and then commented that the presidential election was prejudiced because they only had blacks and whites for candidates. He then asked me what about the Latinos? I told him that since he had so many wonderful qualities that he should run for president. This boy looked at me surprised and then said, "In Mexico, my uncle is president of some company. Maybe I could do something like him." I said, "You better believe that you can, and when you become president, will you take care of the teachers?" He smiled and replied, "Yes."

On a Personal Note...

For myself, I discovered that I have a gift for listening, and being empathetic. At the age of nineteen, I found that I had a gift for working with kids.

Action for the Day

- ✓ Today, make a list of all your gifts and talents. Which special qualities do you bring to the classroom?

6 Seconds Moment

- ◆ Take six seconds to think of one of your talents and how you can magnify it today.

#139.
Life

"We are the living links in a life force that moves and plays around and through us, binding the deepest soils with the farthest stars."
Alan Chadwick

Concept for Today

Many people have unanswered questions regarding their lives. The questions which they ask are usually related to health, money, family, career or love relationships. Think about what is important to you and make categories. For example, my categories include health, family, work, money, spiritual well-being, and relationships. What would your life categories be?

In The Classroom

In the classroom, students come to class with missing links in their categories. As teachers, we do not know what is really going on in the domains of their lives. Students may be living with troubled families, experiencing poverty, hunger, illness, or death. It is our responsibility to provide a safe learning environment with structure, kindness, and consistency. My wish is for students to look forward to coming to school. What is one ritual that would build anticipation for school in our students?

On a Personal Note…

For myself, some of the time, I have trouble in all of my life categories. This is a scary place for me because I can become extremely overwhelmed and despondent. To help counteract these feelings, I like to evaluate my life categories and find one thing that is positive in each.

Action for the Day

- ✓ Today, list the important categories in your life. Think of one upbeat aspect about each domain.

6 Seconds Moment

- ◆ Take six seconds to tell yourself one positive thing that you can do to bring balance when there is trouble in any one of your categories.

#140.
Blaming Others

"To carry a grudge is like being stung to death by one bee."
William Walton

Concept for Today

Have you ever acted like a martyr? I have, many times. When things go wrong, I have blamed others silently and experienced self-pity. Sometimes I have believed that if someone else would just act a certain way, I would be fine. As an adult I finally realize that I have no power or control over others, and that I am responsible for my own actions and feelings. There is no room for either planning recriminations or playing the victim.

In The Classroom

In the classroom, we are trying to provide a quality, well-rounded education. We are also working on teaching our kids self-confidence and self-efficacy. Have you ever had a student who blamed others?

When kids blame others, a major by-product is bitterness. I have witnessed this first hand with a Juvenile Hall student who destroyed the computer mouse after arguing with another student over which song to play. He denied this. Then I told him that I was a witness and proper measures included notifying his mother and probation officer. The boy began to look fearful until I said, "Can you be honest and admit that you destroyed school property? If so, you will receive a lighter consequence. Just take responsibility and be truthful." The boy then admitted to the offense, and sincerely apologized.

I can teach students to become consequential thinkers and to ripple their actions, to ask themselves, "If I do this, what is the first ripple? What might be the second or third ripples?"

On a Personal Note...

For myself, when I start to blame something or someone else, I ask myself what part of the situation is my responsibility.

Action for the Day

- ✓ Today, ask yourself if you blame others. Here is a test: You have worked hard as a teacher and love your school. At the end of the school year, you find out that you will be moving to a school that is not to your liking. What feelings might you have?

6 Seconds Moment

- ◆ Take six seconds to let go of blame.

#141.
Cherish

"Cherish your visions and your dreams as they are the children of your soul; the blueprints of your ultimate achievements."
Napoleon Hill

Concept for Today

What do you hold dear to your heart? Do you have any cherished memories? Are they connected to any one particular person? It is important to think about what you value in life. For the people we value, it is exhilarating to write a simple note to let them know that they are very special to us. When a friend receives a note out of the blue, it is both invigorating and validating.

In The Classroom

In the classroom, what do you appreciate about both your students and your teaching position? Can you think of five things that you treasure about teaching as a career? Would you recommend pursuing a career in teaching to a friend? Why or why not?

On a Personal Note...

For myself, I sometimes forget to let people know how much they are cherished. I need to always remember to say I love you to my family members. I never know what life has in store, and I definitely want my family and friends to know how much I appreciate them. I would be absolutely devastated if my last conversation with a beloved was negative and then something happened to that person.

Action for the Day

- ✓ Today, write down all of the things that you cherish most. Don't forget to celebrate the sunsets, vacations, or holidays.

6 Seconds Moment

- ◆ Take six seconds to make a date to write a personal note to someone special in your life—a note to share that you hold them in the highest esteem.

#142.
Driving

"Leave sooner, drive slower, and live longer."
Anonymous

Concept for Today

Do you remember when you got your driver's license? How did you feel? Do you recall the first time that you drove alone? Do you recollect your first accident? Through the years has your perspective on driving changed?

In The Classroom

In the classroom, I have had the privilege of teaching Driver's Education. I took this responsibility seriously and pushed the idea of caution. I wanted to establish a firm foundation that connects accountability and safety. One day while driving to work, I saw one of my former students speeding by me. He honked the horn and waved exuberantly. I wondered what I had neglected in my lessons.

On a Personal Note…

It is no fun to sit in traffic, pay high gas prices, and encounter others who are in a hurry, or have road rage. It is no fun to drive when I am in a hurry, angry, or when my patience is low. However, I can improve my view of driving as a positive thing by remembering that it is a privilege. I can use the driving experience to practice my patience. Driving can reinforce the concept of living in the moment and concentrating on what you are doing. Driving can be a metaphor for mindfulness. For example, what if, in our own personal lives, we scanned the road ahead for any debris, accidents, or caution areas?

Action for the Day

- ✓ Today, think about your driving. What emotions arise when you are behind the wheel? How can you make your driving experience more positive? How patient are you while driving? Metaphorically, what road are you driving in your own life? Will you travel the road filled with optimism, or the road filled with pessimism?

6 Seconds Moment

- ◆ Take six seconds for a deep breath and focus your mind on the driving task before starting your car, or your day.

#143.
Lighten Up

"Over-seriousness is a warning sign for mediocrity and bureaucratic thinking. People who are seriously committed to mastery and high performance are secure enough to lighten up."
Michael J. Gelb

Concept for Today

Have you ever noticed that many people seem really uptight in this day and age? I have experienced being wrapped so tight that I thought I would scream. Pressures build, communication breaks down, problems multiply, and eventually the dam breaks. Our minds act like noisy radios with nothing but bad news. How do we let it all go and just lighten up?

In The Classroom

I have learned that sometimes simpler is better. I experienced a time when I was trying to be "super teacher." All of my lessons were high intensity teacher support, requiring major planning and extra preparation time. My lessons were consuming a hunk of my personal life and energy. Perhaps I should consider more student-led activities. No one needs or wants a French-fried teacher.

On a Personal Note…

I allow my mind to take a break. I go to my computer and click on YouTube. I play a favorite song, an inspirational teaching, or watch a favorite clip. By just allowing myself to take a mini-vacation, my disposition improves immensely.

Action for the Day

- ✓ Today, let go and lighten up. Ask yourself the question, "How could I lighten up after being pulled over and getting a ticket?"

6 Seconds Moment

- ◆ Take six seconds to make a decision to "lighten up," just for today.

#144.
Body Awareness

"I stand in awe of my body."
Henry David Thoreau

Concept for Today

Have you ever noticed how much tension and stress you carry in your body? Are you aware of the aches and pains that you may be experiencing as a result? Do you brush it off and just keep going like the Energizer bunny? During the first day of a peaceful vacation, it was very surprising for me to realize how tense my body was. I could finally feel my body begin to relax after months of tension. I asked myself why I had to wait so long to pay attention to my physical self. Shouldn't health be a top priority in one's life?

In The Classroom

One of my students was incarcerated for murder. Before I met him, I was a bit intimidated. During our first meeting, I observed this student hunched over, legs and arms crossed, head low. What I saw was a scared little boy. I began talking with him. Slowly, his head began to rise and he began to make eye contact with me. At the end of our conversation, his legs and arms were still crossed, but he had lifted his head and had given me a small smile.

On a Personal Note…

Body awareness is a valuable tool. If there is an ache or pain, I need to pay attention. To locate stress in the body, it is helpful to do a silent assessment from head to toe. I start off by checking in to see how my toes and feet are feeling. As I move up my body, I practice deep breathing and just give a little acknowledgement and appreciation to each part of my body. I want to be in tune with myself.

Action for the Day

- ✓ Today, I will practice paying attention to my body. I will identify and note any stressful, tense parts. I will then devise a mini-treatment for each body part that may be out of whack, whether it be a little massage, a hot bath, or simple stretching.

6 Seconds Moment

- ◆ Take six seconds or longer to do a self-evaluation of all body parts.

#145.
You Are Never Too Old To Play

"A playful path is the shortest road to happiness."
Anonymous

Concept for Today

Do you remember the joy of your childhood experiences? Can you recall playing hide and seek, or Candyland, or perhaps taking a trip to the amusement park? Did your parents ever tell you to go out and play? As adults we may forget to have fun, which can make us gruff, impatient, and deadly serious. The fact is that we are never too old to indulge and practice the art of playing much more regularly.

In The Classroom

Children live in the moment and do not stress on taxes, mortgage payments, or car repairs. Kids look forward to recess, their weekends, and spending time with friends. When it rains, kids play in puddles! As adults, we look ahead to how bad our evening commutes will be. How can we renew our childhood innocence and experience joy no matter what the present circumstances?

On a Personal Note…

For myself, I need to remind myself to be more childlike and to look for moments when play would enliven a lesson. I need to find hands-on activities and manipulatives to bring units "alive". I will make a sincere promise to myself and allow play into life. I will set aside time each day to play with my family. Such playing could include telling jokes, doing a physical activity, or enjoying a board game.

Action for the Day

✓ Today, write down the games that you used to love as a child. What do you discover about yourself from the process? Plan a weekly play date for yourself. As time goes by, incorporate two weekly play dates for yourself.

6 Seconds Moment

◆ Take six seconds to set a date and time to search and find an intriguing educational game for your students.

#146.
Perceive And Receive

"When I perceive each life situation as an opportunity for growth, I receive the gifts and become a stronger human being."
Aline Kaprive

Concept for Today

To perceive means to become aware directly through our senses. When we are truly aware of our present situations we allow ourselves to receive life's gifts. As you go through your day, do you find yourself walking unconsciously or taking in the goodness of each moment?

Do you ever practice "The Six Seconds Model of Know Yourself, Choose Yourself, and Give Yourself?" This model teaches us to truly know ourselves by thoroughly comprehending exactly how we function and increasing our self-awareness; choose ourselves, by intentionally selecting our thoughts, feelings, and actions which strengthen our self-management skills; and give ourselves, by utilizing self-direction, by having empathy, and pursuing our noble goals.

In The Classroom

On one of my busier teaching days, I observed that most of my students were engaged in their science lesson. However, there were a few students who were busy socializing. My first reaction was to get annoyed. I then went over to the students who were chatting, and helped them to get back on task with some words of encouragement. The gift was in watching these previously unfocused kids take their excess energy and direct it to their science assignment. In just one short moment, I had practiced the "Know, Choose, and Give" model. As a result, everybody had benefited.

On a Personal Note...

For myself, I frequently tend to get frustrated by the problem and fail to perceive the situation as a gift. However, with practice, I am beginning to stretch out the moments of opportunity. When I open my senses, and when I stand back and observe, I receive so many gifts.

Action for the Day

- ✓ Today, commit to perceive one situation more objectively. List the gifts that you then receive. This may seem a little awkward, but there is a gift in every irritation if we allow ourselves to search for it.

6 Seconds Moment

- ◆ Take six seconds to stop, perceive the situation, and accurately determine if your action can create a gift for everyone.

#147.
Resiliency

"Our greatest glory is not in never falling, but in rising every time we fall."
Confucius

Concept for Today

Many people are overly sensitive to painful events, and others seem to be born naturally strong and resilient. We have all encountered people who are as strong as locomotives. What skills do they possess when experiencing devastation, ruin, or life's sorrows?

In The Classroom

We must help students to build resiliency skills. We must teach them to have coping methods, which they can use at any time. We can do this in our curricula by sharing literature in which people overcome obstacles, such as Helen Keller adapting to blindness. We can teach a lesson in which students list personal supports, which they can use in case a traumatic event occurs.

On a Personal Note…

For myself, when I was growing up and painful events occurred in my life, I would always break down and cry. If I cried at home, my father told me to stop, or he would give me something to cry about. At school I was very sensitive and would break into tears if kids teased me. This behavior opened the door for more teasing and more tears. I never developed my resiliency skills. Life experience has helped me to develop some resiliency skills but I must remember to continually seek and implement new coping methods.

Action for the Day

- ✓ Today, ask yourself how resilient you are. Rate yourself from one to ten, one being the lowest and ten being the highest. What can you do to raise your score? If a crisis occurred, what would be your coping method? What if three horrible events occurred simultaneously? How would you recover and bounce back?

6 Seconds Moment

- ◆ Take six seconds to think of one positive resiliency skill that you possess and one skill that you can teach your students.

#148.
I See Your Spirit Come Shining Through

"Run your fingers through my soul. For once, just once, feel exactly what I feel, believe what I believe, perceive as I perceive, look, experience, examine, and for once, just once, understand."
Anonymous

Concept for Today

There is nothing in the world more rewarding to me than making a deep connection with a child. Looking past disruptive behaviors, poor grades, color, religion, and personalities provides the opportunity to examine an individual's inner core.

In The Classroom

In the classroom, practice eye contact with all of your students. Look beyond their quirks, idiosyncrasies, and their obstinence. See each child as they truly are, unique and fabulous. Enjoy your co-workers and observe the beauty in each person.

On a Personal Note…

For myself, I have felt a unique relationship bond many times in my life, not only with children but co-workers as well. I can honestly say that I love my students no matter their dispositions. I can arrive at this state by identifying their unique attributes and looking for similar characteristics within myself. With this technique I can establish deeper connections with students, family, and friends. I do not want to judge, but to accept.

Action for the Day

- ✓ Today, look to see the good in all, including people that may "rub you the wrong way." Each day improve upon this practice by making eye contact with people and identifying your commonalities. Write down in your journal when and where you see the goodness in someone else.

6 Seconds Moment

- ◆ Take six seconds to look into someone's eyes and see him/her as a unique individual.

#149.
Awareness

"If we could see the miracle of a single flower clearly, our whole life would change."
Buddha

Concept for Today

I am so thankful when I feel alive, awake, and aware. Unfortunately, so many times, we are not aware of our feelings. The question remains, "How does one become aware or in tune with one's self? How can we slow down to enjoy our surroundings, emotions, and loved ones?" One answer is to breathe, be attentive, and to concentrate.

In The Classroom

As we grow in our teaching, we also seem to develop eyes in the back of our heads and strengthen our hearing. Awareness in the classroom is like driving on the freeway. We are constantly scanning, our radar is up, and we are focused. We pay attention.

On a Personal Note...

For myself, I love to play the awareness game. This is when I deliberately focus on my present surroundings, and tell myself that I am grateful for anyone or anything that is in my presence. Since traffic can stress me out, I practice the awareness game while commuting to work. I recognize the value of the green light, the ease of that day's traffic, the radio in the car, and having a full tank of gas. Try the awareness game; it can help.

Action for the Day

✓ Today, be in tune and aware of your feelings, surroundings, and students. Express appreciation for the multiple "little" things. Write down five things that you are aware of regarding your health, feelings, desires, and thoughts. Write down five positive aspects that are working in your classroom, such as the room set up, curriculum, décor or books.

6 Seconds Moment

◆ Take six seconds to become aware of your current surroundings.

#150.
Tribulations

"The problem is all inside your head, and the answer is easy if you take it logically."
Paul Simon

Concept for Today

Tribulations in life can eat away at us, physically, mentally, and spiritually. How we deal with our afflictions can strengthen our souls and character or destroy us. Sometimes we get so enmeshed and caught up with our troubles that we cannot see the solutions. We need to step back, relax, and reflect. Give a potential solution time to incubate.

In The Classroom

In the classroom, students may come to class with appalling trials, such as neglect, physical abuse, and dysfunctional family situations. I can remember an assignment that an English teacher friend of mine gave. She had her middle school students write letters to Santa stating what they wanted for Christmas. One girl hoped that her parents would not get drunk and quarrel; someone else wished that Santa would bring her absent father home; and another girl hoped that Santa would help her mother get off crack. It amazes me how many challenges our students have already faced in their short lives. We offer stability and provide shoulders to lean on for our students.

On a Personal Note…

For myself, my path has been filled with significant tribulations which never seemed to end. My life has not been easy; however, there are also times of great elation. Life is ever changing and tribulations will pass.

Action for the Day

✓ Today, acknowledge your problems, but spend your energy on the solutions. For the big problems, create a special box and place the troubles inside. Give the solution time to arrive, perhaps in a book, through a friend, etc.

6 Seconds Moment

◆ Take six seconds to acknowledge your biggest problem and tell yourself that the solution is coming.

#151.
Active Intentions

"If it's meant to be, it's up to me."
Terry Gulick

Concept for Today

We have choices throughout our day as to what we could focus upon. There are always stressors to take our attention, or we can deliberately place our intentions on positives. Even if we only think of one thing we commit to doing, we can make a difference. Is there something that can be done, that will make you feel proud and glad that you are a part of the human race? Or are you just coasting through your days? Active intentions that are used for positive outcomes are a precious gift to yourself and others.

In The Classroom

I remind myself regularly to think about children's individual needs. For example, I thought about how one of my students was both a special education student and an English Language learner. I pondered upon him and then, with deliberate intentions put my energy forth to make a difference in his reading program. I pondered, employed creative thought, and walked in on Monday with a plan to make a difference. Ultimately, he improved his reading abilities.

On a Personal Note…

I was once taught a wonderful game by my mother. One day, as we crossed the Golden Gate Bridge and stopped to pay the toll, my mother not only paid her fare but she also paid for the car behind her. The person in that car tried to chase us to say thank you. My mother stepped on the accelerator and sped away before the car could catch us. Throughout my life we have played this game.

What we touch with our focus is either enhanced or depleted by the energy we bring. This is why it is important to keep our lives in a high vibrational place. Allow yourself to be open and alert and allow good things to come your way. Take each moment to be aware of how you are feeling.

Action for the Day

- ✓ Today, take time to think of a deliberately positive intention. Where will you place your energy? Write down five active intentions that can make a difference in your life, as well as your students' lives.

6 Seconds Moment

- ◆ Take six seconds to think about what you intend to do for the next hour, the next day, and the next year.

#152.
Creative Juices

"The creative is the place where no one else has ever been. You have to leave the city of your comfort and go into the wilderness of your intuition. What you'll discover will be wonderful. What you'll discover is yourself."
Alan Alda

Concept for Today

We are so fortunate to be working as teachers because our jobs allow us to be creative and inventive on a daily basis. Do you feel that you are inventive? Do you have any hobbies that allow you to imagine?

In The Classroom

Each day we have the opportunity to take a lesson and add multiple creative components which will spark interest and learning among students. Recently, our school ordered new text books. Along with these textbooks, subject matter CD's also arrived. As I was exploring the CD's, I realized that there were really intriguing art projects accompanying each chapter. Students would not only learn the content but would have the opportunity to express themselves artistically.

What if you are just sick and tired of your lessons? You can restore creativity in the classroom by collaborating with another teacher, searching the internet, going to the library to find books that may give new insight, and calling the curriculum staff at the district. Online, I found a wonderful site called, "The Creative Teacher," which provides lessons and tips to nurture motivations. The first step for replenishing your creativity is to be open to new resources.

On a Personal Note...

There have been times when I felt stagnant. When this happens, I know that I have to take the second step; being open to new experiences. I need to view different scenery, places, and people.

Action for the Day

- ✓ Today, evaluate in what ways you are an innovative person. How do you express your originality in your personal life? When you are burnt out how can you rekindle your inventiveness?

6 Seconds Moment

- ♦ Take six seconds to rank yourself between a one (low) and a ten (high) on your level of creativity. If you have given yourself a low number, what can you do to raise it?

#153. Downtime

"I love that quiet time when nobody's up and the animals are all happy to see me."
Olivia Newton-John

Concept for Today

I need to submerge my mind with downtime. In other words, I must have quiet time, where the focus is not about any difficulties, problems, or pressures. Sometimes life becomes too busy to honor this need. I try to set aside at least a half hour of downtime on weekdays, and more on the weekends, to empty my mind and replenish myself. I may read a good book before bed, take a bath, rest before dinner, walk the dog, not answer my phone for a short period of time, turn off the TV, or lay down on the couch.

In The Classroom

In the classroom, how many times have you completed a lesson and found that there are five or ten minutes left in the class period? How do you handle this downtime? I might play, "Eye-Spy", do a "quick write activity", or have each student share something that they have learned from the lesson. It is extremely important to pace your lessons so you do not fall into the trap of "left-over downtime".

On a Personal Note…

As human beings living in the twenty-first century, we are frequently running on maximum overdrive. By allowing ourselves quiet downtime, we allow our minds and bodies to just be. I need to allow myself to notice the little things: the humming birds in the backyard, the neighbor's roses, the pattering of rain on the roof.

Action for the Day

- ✓ Today, plan some down time just for you. Look at your weekly lesson plan and schedule some down time for students. List some quiet activities that will recharge your batteries. Incorporate one activity into your busy day.

6 Seconds Moment

- ◆ Take six seconds to stop and notice something you usually ignore.

#154.
Uplifting Moments

"Enjoy the little things in life, for one day you may look back and realize they were the big things."
Antonio Smith

Concept for Today

How often do you experience uplifting moments in your life? Remember the moments in which you stood back and said, "Ah ha!" I can recall a wonderful activity in which my professor asked us to reflect upon our lives and find an "Ah ha" moment to share with the class. I appreciated the fact that she asked us to do this during the middle of the semester, as there needs to be a sense of community established before one can share an intimate moment like this. I also liked the fact that we had time to reflect in order to choose our favorite. What was illuminating about this exercise was that the preparation led to discovering how many "Ah ha" moments I had.

In The Classroom

In the classroom, after a cooperative community has been established, this magical "Ah ha" lesson allows students to discover and compare similarities and differences. You can spread this activity out and have a few students share each day. It is a wonderful way to start your class and works with all age groups.

On a Personal Note...

For myself, it is fascinating to reflect upon the uplifting moments of my life. For the above class, I chose to share about meeting my biological father for the first time when I was twenty-nine years old. The process of choosing a favorite moment and then sharing it, and receiving constructive feedback generates a significant increase in trust in the classroom community. How do you give constructive feedback on a personal note?

Action for the Day

- ✓ Today, reflect upon the "Ah ha" moments that you have experienced. Try to find a humorous one, an emotional one, and a physical one. Or identify one for each of the seven major emotions: sadness, joy, anger, fear, disgust, surprise, and anticipation.

6 Seconds Moment

- ◆ Take six seconds to pick an uplifting moment in your life to share with a trusted friend or relative.

#155. Endless Refreshment

"Silence is refreshment for the soul."
Wynonna Judd

Concept for Today

Think of yourself stranded in the desert. What does your body crave the most? The answer is probably water. Picture how good it feels to drink water when you are dehydrated. What would life be like if each person were endlessly refreshed mentally, physically, and emotionally? How can we keep our lives filled with continuous refreshment?

In The Classroom

I have observed that teachers tend to verbalize exhaustion in March, as they wait for the spring break. I wanted to know how to keep myself refreshed during the seemingly endless segments of teaching without a vacation. The answer came in the form of careful curriculum planning. During these long periods, I would schedule field trips, assemblies, and guest speakers. These events offered a new element in the classroom. My students were still learning wonderful material with the structure and delivery handled in a more unique manner. By easing up on my intense lessons and offering fresh learning experiences, both my students and I were more engaged.

On a Personal Note...

For myself, my wish would be to feel endlessly refreshed. One way to do this is to wake up thinking the day is crisp and new. Moreover, there are things that I can do to refresh myself, such as drinking plenty of water, getting extra rest, changing my routine just a little, changing my hair-do, going to a new restaurant, or making a new friend. The point is to change my routine, a little or a lot.

Action for the Day

- ✓ Today, think about how you can refresh your life and spirit. Make a list of five ways to change your daily schedule, both at school and at home.

6 Seconds Moment

- ◆ Take six seconds to decide how you might help refresh someone else's day.

#156. Another's Eyes

"One should never criticize his own work except in a fresh and hopeful mood. The self-criticism of a tired mind is suicide."
Charles Horton

Concept for Today

We tend to be very self-critical and probably would never talk to a friend the way we talk to ourselves. For example, what would a treasured friend say about you? How do other people see you? What might your significant other say about you? Think about teacher observations completed by the principal. What do they reveal? I have always appreciated doing professor evaluations at the end of each semester in college and also want feedback from my students, no matter their age. Don't you love it when students say that you have inspired them or taught them something new?

In The Classroom

A great activity is to have students draw a self-portrait and write words that describe themselves. Encourage students to dig deep. When they complete the assignment, write ten positive comments on the back. After classroom trust and community have been established, write the names of each student on a sheet of paper and pass this around for positive comments from their classmates.

On a Personal Note…

For myself, I have often worried about what other people think. Perhaps they will not like me or judge me. I understand how a teenager might feel when it comes to fitting in with peers. Developing and maintaining a healthy self-concept is a mandatory skill for Life: 101.

Action for the Day

- ✓ Today, write the following words on a paper: friend, parent, spouse, boss, co-worker, child, significant other or mate. Think about what these people would say about you. Ask them for feedback and absorb their valued comments.

6 Seconds Moment

- ◆ Take six seconds to compliment a friend about one of their outstanding characteristics.

#157.
Teacher Credentialing

"Nothing could be worse than the fear that one had given up too soon, and left one unexpended effort that might have saved the world."
Jane Adams

Concept for Today

Do you remember your sense of pride after earning your credential? It was a successful struggle fueled by perseverance and commitment. I wonder why teachers do not frame their credentials and hang them in their classrooms. It says volumes about you. When you receive your credential, the state allows you to teach youth. What an honor! (How many hours of endless studying, researching, tests, and student teaching did you put in?) Pat yourself on the back because you never gave up.

In The Classroom

I am always guiding students to dream "bodaciously" when it comes to education and future. I recently taught an innovative history lesson on the importance of a high school diploma and posed the question, "Is it worth all of the time, effort, and money?" Students researched careers, statistics, and salaries to draw their own conclusions. To emotionally hook students, I made little diplomas wrapped with ribbon. Students reached consensus that a high school diploma, then a college degree, were the best options for their futures.

On a Personal Note...

For myself, I attended college late in life. At the age of thirty, I had only forty college credits. I desperately wanted to be a teacher. When I did in fact complete the program, I felt discouraged because I had only earned my preliminary credential and had to complete two additional years of "Beginning Teacher Support and Assessment Induction" before I could become fully qualified. The rigorous process was necessary to graduate highly qualified teachers. However, I worry that credential students will find the process too difficult.

Action for the Day

- ✓ Today, celebrate your credential. Think about the blood, sweat, time, and tears that went into it. If you are now in the credential program yourself, what do you do to take care of yourself? To persevere?

6 Seconds Moment

- ◆ Take six seconds to reflect on your credential and pat yourself on the back.

#158.
Fear

"Only when we are no longer afraid do we begin to live."
Dorothy Thompson

Concept for Today

Everyone has fears in their life. How do you face your fears? Do you have a set process in which you step up and face your fear courageously? Do you hold onto any irrational fear? Fear can have two usages: "Forget Everything and Run", or "Face Everything and Recover". Which meaning do you practice in your own life?

In The Classroom

In the classroom, I often see the results of gangs and bullying. Students have shared with me that they have to join a gang for protection. They then choose to bully rather than be bullied because of gang initiation rites. One of my student gang members desperately wanted to find a way out. He and I decided that more education was one way to cope and worked on getting him away from his neighborhood. He decided to apply to an out-of-state college. It worked.

On a Personal Note…

For myself, I have lived in fear for most of my life. I was afraid to speak up, afraid to take risks, afraid of making mistakes, and am still afraid of losing my beloved grandmother. I also possess irrational fears such as driving over bridges and encountering rodents. Fear can create cages from which it is difficult to escape.

Action for the Day

- ✓ Today, make a list of your fears. Are they rational or irrational? Ask yourself if you face fear, or run from it.

6 Seconds Moment

- ♦ Take six seconds to identify one fear. Make a commitment to face it for today.

#159.
Time Management

"Today, be aware of how you are spending your 1,440 beautiful moments, and spend them wisely."
Anonymous

Concept for Today

In the twenty-first century, busy people believe that there is not enough time. How can we accomplish all of the necessary tasks throughout the day? We always seem to be rushing and, as a result, suffer from "hurry sickness." There is always work, family, kids, bills, household chores, shopping, errands, and even social responsibilities. How can we eliminate hurry sickness?

In The Classroom

In the classroom, to manage the demands of teaching, it is very helpful to take responsibilities and assignments and break them down into manageable tasks. Suppose you need to correct one hundred papers within two days. Try breaking the chore into two increments of forty-five minute blocks each day. Perhaps you have to create an individual reading program for an English Language Learner. Set a deadline for completion and then work on the project task for one half-hour each day. If you have phone calls to make, set aside a specific time. Working chunks of time reduces stress and helps you to build forward momentum.

On a Personal Note…

My personal time-management system is to make a daily list and identifying items as either A, B, or C. I commit to all items marked "A" and re-evaluate the B's and C's each day. Some "C" items I have yet to finish. And yes–sometimes I do work during lunch.

Action for the Day

✓ Today, think about how you manage your time. Write down several suggestions for improvement. If a new teacher comes to you overwhelmed with the workload of teaching, what advice would you give him or her?

6 Seconds Moment

◆ Take six seconds to affirm to yourself that you can establish a system of tasks to accomplish and still have time for yourself.

#160.
Scrumditiliumptius Inside And Out

"Chocolate kisses and ice cream wishes add to my sweetness every day."
Sarah Hammer

Concept for Today

Do you recall reading the book or seeing the movie, "Charlie and the Chocolate Factory" written by Roald Dahl? In both, Willie Wonka has created a chocolate bar called "Scrumditiliumptius." What a great word! What do you picture in your mind? Perhaps the words yummy, divine, luscious, mouthwatering, etc. provide a context. As adults, it is important to feel "scrumditiliumptius" from head to toe. We need to tap into our inner selves and occasionally acknowledge our inner child.

In The Classroom

How often do you and your students feel "scrumditiliumptious" about learning? Isn't it just fabulous to see a student laugh and enjoy your lessons? I recall a wonderful professor who used to begin the class by having students tell a joke. Often, when I began teaching, I would utilize this method. Other times, I would write a riddle on the board and simply allow students to try and solve it.

For a writing prompt, I like to have students think of their favorite candy and write down adjectives to describe it. I then ask kids to compare themselves to the candy. They can use a Venn diagram while they list similarities and differences. Hopefully, with this activity kids will recognize that they are "scrumditiliumptius."

On a Personal Note…

There are still times when I feel "tickled-pink" or "scrumditiliumptius." For example, surprises make me feel this way. Unexpected compliments do this. And "I love you, Mom," from my daughter always does this.

Action for the Day

- ✓ Today, write down the word "scrumditiliumptius" and see what definitions come to mind. How often do you feel this way? Defining a day as this way allows positive things to come your way.

6 Seconds Moment

- ◆ Take six seconds to affirm that you are "scrumditiliumptius" from head to toe.

#161.
Voice

"Lower your voice and strengthen your argument."
Lebanese Proverb

Concept for Today

What type of voice do you have? Is it soprano, tenor, bass, or alto? Do you enjoy singing? Our voices are special tools which can be used to better express who we are to the world. We can mutter or roar of articulate justice, or divulge our feelings.

In The Classroom

Do you use your voice to enhance your lesson presentation and establish classroom management? I have found that one of the best techniques in classroom management is to speak softly. When a child is engaging in behavior that is not positive, I give a calm warning. I try never to yell and embarrass the child. When I am trying to get students' attention, I simply stand in front of the class and quietly say, "I'll wait." Within a minute or so, students settle down. If a student is engaging in a negative behavior, I write a warning on a post-it and place it on their desk. I then make a gesture for quiet.

Think about your voice when you deliver a lesson. Do you remember to change your pitch? I strive to remember that I am often the *only* support to speak on behalf of my students. It is also essential to teach young people to recognize that they have their own voices and that they can be effective self-advocates.

On a Personal Note…

I have learned to take all situations less seriously, and disengage when conflict arises. I no longer am tempted to yell.

Action for the Day

- ✓ Today, ask yourself how effective your voice is in classroom management. Do you use your voice to bring about positive circumstances in your life?

6 Seconds Moment

- ◆ Take six seconds to plan a "voice action" that will promote hope for another.

#162.
Can-Do Attitude

"Whether you think you can or think you can't - you are right."
Henry Ford

Concept for Today

When we are little, we believe in ourselves as successful. I recall my fifth grade teacher asking us what we would be doing in the year 2000. I remember writing that I would live in Arizona, own a beautiful home, and be a water ski instructor. As I made my future plans, there was absolutely no self-doubt regarding the pursuit of my dreams. As I grew older, experiences brought self-doubt. I lost a "can-do" attitude. I discovered that self-confidence needs to be bolstered daily.

In The Classroom

It is delightful to work with elementary-aged children. They are confident, enthusiastic, and want to succeed. It is important to build upon their self-assuredness. The adolescent years bring about self-doubt, awkwardness, and a deep longing to be accepted. How can we instill a "can-do" attitude in our kids? It is important to make each student feel unique and to regularly offer them praise for specific accomplishments.

I remember my attitude when I failed my teacher's subject-matter test three times. I studied harder and took my "can-do" attitude into the testing situation. By focusing all of my energy on passing the test, I achieved my dream of becoming a teacher.

On a Personal Note...

When I look back, I wonder what I could have done differently to help build my self-confidence along the way. I do believe that I could have maintained more positive interactions with peers if I had put on my "emotional raincoat" when I was teased and ridiculed in middle school. Surviving this time, I began to appreciate myself. Now, in my forties, I still work on maintaining a "can-do" attitude.

Action for the Day

- ✓ Today, make a decision to practice "can-do-ness" in all of your affairs. Develop an exuberant strength of mind and persist with your greatest dreams.

6 Seconds Moment

- ◆ Take six seconds to remind yourself that you *can* do it!

#163.
Flowered Underpants

"Such embarrassing moments make you want to hide your face in the ground. But these moments become memorable anecdotes that you will one day share with your grandkids."
Simran Khurana

Concept for Today

Many times I have heard my friends and acquaintances declare that high school was one of the happiest and most memorable times in their lives. One reason that I chose to teach at-risk teenagers was because I knew that their past school experiences were anything but positive. My hope was to help these kids fall in love with learning and to change the direction of their lives.

An embarrassing moment I can recall as a fifteen-year old started with wearing white slacks to school. The teacher asked me to go up to the board and solve a math problem. The only thing that I heard were the kids laughing at me. All of the kids could see my flowered underwear through my white slacks. How humiliating! Wouldn't it be nice if school were a safe place where students would not be ridiculed, and harassed?

In The Classroom

We all have "flowered underpants" stories in our past school experiences. When a teenager experiences an embarrassing moment the feeling is intensified one-thousand times. What can we do to help our kids through the rough times and stop the harassing and teasing?

On a Personal Note…

There was one evening when I heard my daughter crying. She revealed that she was absolutely miserable at her new school and had no friends. She had been working in a small math group and told me how cruel the other group members were to her. What shocked me was the fact that I, as a parent, missed the signs of how much emotional pain my daughter was experiencing. It also amazed me that her algebra teacher had missed the signs of cruelty occurring in the small groups. Are we so busy that we forget to notice how other human beings are feeling?

Action for the Day

- ✓ Today, make a conscious, heartfelt decision to become more aware. If you utilize small group instruction, make sure that rules are established and that all learners are safe.

6 Seconds Moment

- ◆ Take six seconds today to closely observe your class. Ask yourself if you think any student is being harassed or bullied.

#164.
The Plague

"Gossip is sometimes referred to as halitosis of the mind."
Anonymous

Concept for Today

Negativity, gossip, conflicts, personality clashes, and hurt feelings can spread like the plague. Have you ever worked in a hurtful environment? Have you ever felt that you must walk on egg shells around other people? What do you do when you are surrounded by negative people? While at work, have you ever heard someone say that the people on the job act like they are still in high school?

In The Classroom

I have witnessed students gossiping, not getting along, and acting petty. How can we help our students learn respect and kindness toward all other human beings? There is no doubt in my mind that there will always be conflicts; however, the question becomes how can we teach our students to deal with these situations? It seems to me that the classroom is a microcosm of the real world. We have to teach our students to get along with one another, and rise above their differences. I give my students a basic tool set that includes these five emotional intelligence competencies: self-awareness, self-regulation, self-motivation, empathy, and skills for developing nurturing relationships.

On a Personal Note…

I try to act as a role model for my students by not engaging in negative, gossiping behaviors. I teach my students to be considerate and allow other people their feelings. I also encourage them to set boundaries and not to be drawn into negativity. I help them realize that "it takes two" to make a smile, and if their smile is ignored by another, then try again.

Action for the Day

- ✓ Today, ask yourself what your behavior is when it comes to "warring with words." How do you teach your students to be kind to one another?

6 Seconds Moment

- ◆ Take six seconds to commit to walking away from gossip at your job.

#165.
Loving Myself

"I love myself, therefore I..."
Louise Hay

Concept for Today

Can you complete the title of this passage written by Louise Hay? What would your answer be? How often do you think about loving yourself unconditionally? What does your inner dialogue say? Do you remember to think thoughts of love, or are you filled with worry, resentment, or stress?

In The Classroom

We start by loving ourselves and taking care of our needs. Love is endless and the more love that we give ourselves, the more we have for others. Many teachers might think that their classrooms are not a place for love, but ask yourself if you teach from a condition of emotional unavailability. I work in Juvenile Hall and must maintain discipline, order, and structure. This does not mean that I cannot come from a place of love. I manage my class with justice, equity, and care. Most of my students have never had a kind teacher and truly appreciate it.

On a Personal Note…

I complete the sentence, "I love myself, therefore I… am cheerful. I love myself, therefore I am compassionate. I love myself, therefore I am optimistic. I love myself, therefore I laugh. I love myself, therefore I am capable of endurance."

When negative thoughts, stress, or chaos engulfs me, I repeat the sentence with multiple new endings. It empowers me and brings me back to what is important and significant in my life.

Action for the Day

✓ Today, finish the sentence with six positive responses. I love myself, therefore I….

6 Seconds Moment

◆ Take six seconds to finish the sentence with an attribute you want to share.

#166. Acceptance

"The truth is I can find no serenity until I accept that person, place, thing, or situation as being exactly the way it is supposed to be at this moment. I need to accept life completely on life's terms."
Big Book of Alcoholics Anonymous, 4th edition

Concept for Today

There is no doubt that life is tough. There have been so many times in which I blamed others, or blamed my circumstances, parents, or life itself. I did not realize that I have absolutely no control over other people. The only thing that I can possibly change is my attitude. Our cups are either half empty or half full. It is a relief to accept people and situations as they are. Total acceptance is truly a key to my tranquility.

In The Classroom

There was a year in which I felt that I had been given the worst teaching assignment, lousiest location, and the most difficult students and parents. I certainly had a million reasons to justify my concern. The previous teacher had quit after only one day. The parents had sued the school district the previous year. Thankfully, the kids made considerable progress, the parents were pleased, and I even earned my Master's degree. Please understand that some days I cried on the way to work because this job was so difficult. Luckily, I did not wallow too long. Instead, I accepted my situation and grew tremendously, both personally and professionally.

On a Personal Note...

I can only control my actions, and thoughts. Self-pity is useless and blaming others is a waste of time. Believe me I am still learning these lessons.

Action for the Day

- ✓ Today, think about how total acceptance of a tough situation can set you free. Brainstorm how you can change your attitude, and generate solutions.

6 Seconds Moment

- ◆ Take six seconds to affirm that you will accept things as they are and work on creative responses.

#167.
Blank Page

"The pages are still blank, but there is a miraculous feeling of the words being there, written in invisible ink and clamoring to become visible."
Vladimir Nabakov

Concept for Today

Imagine discovering a book written about your life. What would the theme and setting be? What stories and places would be included? What characters would play important roles in your story? Are there antagonists and heroes? Is there suspense, laughter, romance, adventure, and excitement? Are there joyful and melancholy episodes? If you left this earth and someone discovered your book, would they enjoy reading it?

In The Classroom

It is extremely important for students to write on a daily basis. Perhaps you provide a time for journaling and free writing. Journaling relieves stress, and free writing opens the door for creative expression, as well as emotional release. When students journal, and share their inner selves with you on paper, a trusting bond is established. Journaling allows students to write their dreams and goals. There is power in the pen, and writing aspirations down on paper establishes a realistic concreteness.

On a Personal Note…

For myself, I recall going through dark times in my life and being advised to write down my troubles before I went to sleep. This ritual allowed me to let go of the noisy, stressful thoughts which always tended to haunt me during the night.

Action for the Day

✓ Today, think about how you incorporate writing, journaling, and diary keeping in your classroom. Is this a classroom ritual? How do you help students fall in love with writing? Do you use student writing samples for portfolios?

6 Seconds Moment

◆ Take six seconds to think about yourself as a writer. Ask yourself if journaling can be an emotional release.

#168.
Help And Support

"I came upon a man who appeared in quite poor health. I said, "There's nothing that I can do for you that you can't do for yourself.' He said, 'Oh yes, you can. Just hold my hand. So I sat with him a while... 'He said, 'I think I'm cured.'"
Conor Oberst

Concept for Today

It is essential to ask for help. It does not make us inferior. Do you seek help and support, or do you like to work alone? If you make a mistake, are you the first to admit it, or do you hope that no one will notice?

In The Classroom

Many students will not ask for help. They do not want to appear unintelligent in front of their classmates and so may prefer to do an assignment incorrectly. It may be a challenge for some students to raise their hands and admit that they do not understand the task. How can you establish a trusting relationship and help students to open up? One answer is to provide a safe classroom that is a pleasant place to be. Or have a one-on-one conference with a hesitant student. Treat all individuals with respect and with courtesy. Our students may ask for help if they perceive we are willing to give it.

On a Personal Note…

For myself, as a child, I can remember being laughed at by my peers. I also had teachers who were sarcastic and rejecting. As a result, I never wanted to raise my hand in class. One of my most embarrassing moments was roll call. My name is Aline, but absolutely no teacher could pronounce it correctly (AI-LEEN). When the teacher read the roll, and butchered my name, the students always laughed. The result is that today I have zero tolerance for embarrassment of students. Now, when people mispronounce my name, I stand up and speak assertively and tell them that my name is pronounced like Eileen but with a strong "A" spelled Aline. I am helping myself by being assertive.

Action for the Day

- ✓ Today, ask yourself if you seek help when needed.

6 Seconds Moment

- ◆ Take six seconds to remind yourself to promote an "accepting attitude" in your classroom.

#169.
Integrity

"To reach a great height a person needs to have great depth."
Anonymous

Concept for Today

To reach new heights in our day-to-day lives, we need to evaluate the depths of our souls and examine our values. What values and characteristics make up the foundation of who you are? Through adversity, pain, and suffering, I came to understand what values were most important to me. I knew that if I wanted to reach the sky and have my dreams fulfilled, I needed to have a healthy foundation filled with the positive values of care, kindness, compassion, and altruism.

In The Classroom

In the classroom, one of the greatest difficulties of teaching high school students is helping to establish values. Many of my students believe that stealing, lying, and violence are the way to survive. One fabulous activity which can be used in the classroom is the Value Sort Experiment from Self-Science: The Emotional Intelligence Curriculum. Students are given eight cards with different values written on them and their task is to sort and rate the cards. Number one is the value that is most important to them. And eight is the least important. This activity can be done in small groups or individually. Having taught this lesson many times, it always amazes me that even the most hard core gang members rate family as number one. This tells me that it is never too late to reinforce the values of family, peace, and friendship.

On a Personal Note…

During my adolescent years, my values were distorted and therefore my integrity was in jeopardy. I indulged in behaviors that did not reflect the real me. I had a few physical fights as a teenager, cut school, and participated in some risky behavior. These behaviors left me emotionally, spiritually, and physically bankrupt. I realized that I needed to perform some good deeds to balance my bank account. Now that my values are in order, I am happier.

Action for the Day

- ✓ Today, ask yourself if you have integrity. Has there ever been a time when you did not have integrity and made poor choices? How does your integrity display itself in your daily behaviors?

6 Seconds Moment

- ◆ Take six seconds to assess the level of integrity in your life.

#170.
Hearts And Minds

"Be aware of wonder. Live a balanced life— learn some and think some and draw and paint and sing and dance and play and work every day some."
Robert Fulgham

Concept for Today

When you do things truly from the heart, life will unfold in a magnificent way. When you do things on an intellectual level, wisdom will strengthen your decisions and experiences. When you align "brain + heart", you will find a balanced result for a life filled with bright ideas, confident decision making, and love.

In The Classroom

We can help our students to develop both their hearts and brains. When implementing a lesson, begin with an emotional hook, such as showing a picture, doing a merry-go-round walk, (which assesses student background knowledge), or asking an engaging question. Then throughout the lesson boost thinking skills such as analysis, sequencing, and logic. Each lesson will contain innovative learning, creativity, imagination, and exploration. It takes planning to implement a lesson that utilizes the mind and heart, however the results are phenomenal.

On a Personal Note…

When I was in my late teens, people used to tell me that I had a fantastic, logical mind. I was a great problem solver and planner. As life went on, when problems arose, I would behave emotionally rather than rationally. I found myself being an emotional wreck rather than a reasonable and logical person. Gradually, each day became a little better and I found myself utilizing my intelligence and regulating my emotions. I still have slips, but after calming down and reflecting, I can use my mind and my heart.

Action for the Day

- ✓ Today, ask yourself how your heart and mind function together.

6 Seconds Moment

- ◆ Take six seconds to evaluate a problem and ask yourself whether your mind or heart guides your thoughts, reactions, and outcomes.

#171.
The Despicable, Horrible, Rotten, No Good, Very Bad Day

"You know it's a bad day when you put your bra on backwards and it fits better."
Anonymous

Concept for Today

How often have you had days in which everything went wrong? How do you deal with those days? I wonder if our thoughts have anything to do with this domino effect. If we think that it is going to be a despicable, horrible, rotten, no good, very bad day, chances are it will be. You wake up late, you hit every red light, your car runs out of gas, the boss yells at you, you forget your lesson plan, the kids are unruly, and your day just gets worse and worse. You come home from work and there is nothing for dinner, your child is cranky, your finance company calls because your car payment is overdue, the computer has crashed, and your dog has chewed your new shoes.

In The Classroom

I enjoy reading, "Alexander and The Terrible, Horrible, No Good, Very Bad Day" by Judith Viorst. I then ask the students to write their own "very-bad-day" story. To add optimism to the unit, I then turn the tables and have students write a story about themselves and "a very-good-day". This story works well with students of all ages.

On a Personal Note…

I knew that it was going to be a terrible, horrible, no good, very bad day, when I overslept since I had forgotten to set the timer the night before, could not find my car keys, and discovered that there was no coffee. While fixing the coffee, I motivated myself to turn the day around by repeating over and over that "it would be a very good day". Repeating this mantra changed my attitude. Changing my attitude changed my day.

Action for the Day

- ✓ Today, write about a time when everything went wrong. How did you feel? Can you laugh about it now?

6 Seconds Moment

- ◆ Take six seconds to create a mantra that will strengthen your determination to have positive days.

#172.
Crazy Hair Day

"It's not the hair on your head that matters. It's the kind of hair you have inside."
Gary Shandling

Concept for Today

Do you like your hair? Does it cooperate? Mine has a mind of its own. Some days I like my hair and other days, "yuck!" Being a teacher means usually buying the cheaper brands of hair products. However, it is important to go ahead and splurge once in a while. Celebrate yourself by occasionally purchasing the more expensive brands.

In The Classroom

Does your school ever have spirit days? Students really seem to enjoy them, and it brings about a sense of school unity. My favorite spirit day was crazy hair day. My daughter was really excited about this opportunity. I took her long, blonde hair and ratted it, and proceeded to spray on the "temporary" hot pink dye. She looked as if she had bubble gum in her hair. Crazy hair day was a success. However, when I came home from a long day at school, my husband was furious! Our bathtub was bright pink, and there were stained towels, and pink all over the shower tiles. I went into my daughter's bedroom and there was pink on her sheets and pillow cases. I honestly never wanted to see pink "not so temporary" dye again.

On a Personal Note…

It is essential that I save extra money to spend on my appearance. Of course I do not go crazy spending on myself, but every once in a while, splurge! If I do not like something about my appearance, I can change it.

Action for the Day

- ✓ Today, ask yourself if you like your hair and your overall appearance. How often do you spend money on yourself, just for the heck of it? Make a "to feel special" list of ten positive things about yourself.

6 Seconds Moment

- ◆ Take six seconds to admire your hair, eyes, and smile.

#173.
Life Maps

"Your goals are the road maps that guide you and show you what is possible for your life."
Les Brown

Concept for Today

If you were to draw a map of your life, what would it look like? What key people, defining moments, and geographical places stand out on your map?

In The Classroom

I have my students create life maps. They draw a road and mark the significant events that have occurred throughout their lives. These "life maps" are an opportunity to reflect on the past and plan for the future.

On a Personal Note...

For myself, I have created my own life map. As I look back and reflect, I believe that I am meant to be here on this planet bringing optimism and hope to my fellow human beings. At age one and a half, I had a close call with death. I am not sure what happened but I fell out of a two story window and cracked my head on the sidewalk. My mother and grandmother rushed me to the hospital. My life is a miracle.

Since I escaped death, I want to make sure my life stands for something. I look back and it appears that everything happened as it was supposed to. My life unfolded in a unique and personal way. Each event has built upon the next. For example, when I was nineteen years old, a friend at college told me about a job as a recreation leader. I decided to fill out the application, just for the heck of it. Two weeks later, I was called in for an interview. Again, just for the heck of it, I went. I obtained the job and fell in love with the kids. I found out by accident that I was meant to work with children. Helping troubled youth discover they can change their lives became my "noble goal."

Action for the Day

✓ Today, draw your own life map.

6 Seconds Moment

◆ Take six seconds to think about the ultimate purpose of your life. What is your "noble goal?"

#174.
Got Spunk?

"The road to success can be rediscovered if you learn to overcome your obstacles with spunk."
L. Dianne Wolfe

Concept for Today

How spunky are you? Do you think of yourself as timid or fearless? Every time you face and overcome a challenge, you build your spunk and develop more steel in your backbone.

In The Classroom

It is amazing to observe kids who have spunk, spirit, and courage. I can recall working with a girl who had multiple disabilities. At birth, the doctors predicted a short life span. Amazingly, this little girl is now twenty-one years old and is attending community college. I asked her parents to share her secret and they told me that she is too stubborn, high-spirited, and ornery to allow her disabilities to get the best of her.

On a Personal Note…

As a child, I lacked spunk. In my home, if I ever questioned my father's authority, I received the belt. This diminished my spirit and I went through life afraid of everyone and everything. As a result, I became a victim of bullying. At fourteen, I fought back when a girl came at me with violent force. The fighting was so vicious that the security guard kicked us both out of the mall. Later, I discovered that this girl attacked me because she was trying to earn her spot in a gang. She had to beat someone up and she had chosen me since I appeared so weak and scared.

After that, I knew that I could stand up for myself. I had found my "line in the sand." I am not suggesting that fighting is the answer, and believe me I was terrified. However, I learned that I had spunk when I needed it.

Action for the Day

- ✓ Today, think of a time in your life when you showed your spunk. What happened? Do you believe that your actions were appropriate? Is this a story to share with your friends and family?

6 Seconds Moment

- ◆ Take six seconds to appreciate one of your "spunky" students or a student without spunk, and consider how you might help them. Are they really afraid? Can you help them overcome the fear?

#175.
Salary Issues

"The real measure of your wealth is how much you'd be worth if you lost all your money."
Anonymous

Concept for Today

It is unbelievable to me that teachers are still underpaid for the valuable service which they provide. Teachers are dedicated champions who truly love helping kids to grow.

In The Classroom

It is important to teach students about money–working within a budget and acquiring the life skills necessary for managing savings and checking accounts plus credit cards and bills. Being intelligent about managing money should be a required course. As a teacher, think of ways to incorporate a money unit into your curriculum.

On a Personal Note…

Salary was not the top priority in choosing my career. However, as many teachers do, I have tried to supplement my salary by substituting at the adult school, working as a tutor, and performing respite work; i.e., relief for a family with a special needs child. There are many things that can be done to supplement one's salary, if we think creatively. I recall a math teacher working as a tutor to finance a higher degree and a PE teacher working part time at the community college in order to fund his daughter's college degree. Remember, we have a gift that can be used as a source of income.

Action for the Day

- ✓ Today, evaluate your salary. Is it enough to live on? Ask yourself what you do during the summer months for income. Think of three part-time jobs that you would enjoy and could help your income. Keep in mind to check higher-paying districts, just in case you need a change and a higher wage.

6 Seconds Moment

- ◆ Take six seconds to think of one reason that you have chosen the teaching profession, even though the salaries are low.

#176.
Teacher Burn-out

"Burn-out can lead to negative scenarios such as emotional exhaustion, stress, and "zombie-esque" feelings."
Mark Dumon

Concept for Today

For the first time in my teaching career, I felt unenthusiastic about starting the new school year. Right then and there, I made a conscious decision to not cheat my students, but to do whatever it took to rev myself up. First, I watched several videos that demonstrated new teaching strategies and provided some inspiration. I also ordered a new piece of technology, a Smart Board, and researched how this equipment could strengthen my lessons. I felt ready to go in and do what I loved, which was to teach. By sparking my creative juices, I walked into the classroom ready to rock and roll.

In The Classroom

I decided that my first week would be filled with fun, games, and new projects. Another way to rejuvenate yourself is to advise a colleague who is less experienced than you. Or you could call the local university and speak to a professor about volunteering to share your experiences with credential seeking students. Perhaps one of them needs a mentor.

On a Personal Note...

I need to remember to take time frequently for self-rejuvenation and to reflect upon why I entered the education field.

Action for the Day

- ✓ Today, make a plan to prevent burn-out. What will you do to re-kindle your spirit and creativity?

6 Seconds Moment

- ◆ Take six seconds to research one new tool, technique, or resource that will enliven your job.

#177. Mustaches

"I had beautiful wavy hair and a waxed mustache."
Curly Howard

Concept for Today

Mustaches do not seem to be as popular as they once were. Mustaches on ladies have never been popular. High school students notice everything about their teacher's appearance. Younger children are also quite observant and will show no restraint when commenting on it. If you are a lady teacher, and have a mustache, they will be eager to point it out.

In The Classroom

Once, there was a time when a mustache helped an absenteeism problem. I was working as an aide in an alternative school. Our attendance was absolutely terrible. In order to correct this problem, the principal told the students that he would shave his head and his mustache, if perfect attendance occurred for one month. The students rose to the challenge and met the goal. So, during morning announcements, the principal came out and shaved his beloved mustache and hair. The students applauded enthusiastically. I really appreciated that our principal was creative and motivated the students in a unique and unusual way. I also applaud his commitment to his promise.

On a Personal Note...

I have to rise above worrying about mustaches, and other personal imperfections, while standing in front of students. Instead, I take risks and draw attention to myself by dressing up for Halloween, coming in costume to do a story presentation, dressing in green for Saint Patrick's Day, or wearing bright pink and red on Valentine's Day. Students love the occasional wacky behavior, and see me as a friendly and personal instructor.

Action for the Day

- ✓ Today, write down the risks that you might take while teaching. If your students have poor attendance and meet a goal of perfect attendance for one month, would you volunteer to shave your head?

6 Seconds Moment

- ◆ Take six seconds to think of a risk you could take tomorrow. Tie it to a goal your students need to reach.

#178.
Our Make-Up

"Our character is but the stamp on our souls of the free choices of good and evil we have through life."
John C. Geikie

Concept for Today

All of our past experiences, mistakes, victories, trials, and tribulations make us the people we are today. If you had a painful childhood, does it reflect in the adult that you have become? If you were bullied are you now a wishy-washy person? If you were raised by loving, positive parents, does this make you a more generous and compassionate individual? If you have children, are you raising them the way that you were raised or trying new methods? Do you think that you have any character defects such as stinginess, control issues, self-centeredness, a short temper, dishonesty, or cowardliness?

In The Classroom

Each teacher brings his or her own personality and life experiences. What makes one teacher stand out more than another? During my college days, I can recall that everyone had a favorite professor named Arabella. This makes me wonder what past experiences made her the wonderful teacher that she is today. What experiences do you bring to your students? What if you never learned to deal with responsibility? What if you have little patience or cope with anger through sarcasm? Does that flow out into the classroom?

On a Personal Note…

For myself, I hated some parts of my childhood and past. I had resentment, and anger. I also had triumphs as well as failures, beautiful loving relationships, joy, and excitement. All of my past experiences make up the woman that I am today.

Action for the Day

- ✓ Today, analyze and evaluate your own assets and defects. What can you do to reduce the defects and magnify the assets? What life experiences, knowledge, gifts, and wisdom do you have to offer your students?

6 Seconds Moment

- ◆ Take six seconds to write three assets that you possess. Post them on your rear view mirror.

#179.
Emotional Intelligence

"A man who is master of himself can end a sorrow as easily as he can invent a pleasure. I don't want to be at the mercy of my emotions. I want to use them, to enjoy them, and to dominate them."
Oscar Wilde

Concept for Today

People rush through life and often do not recognize how they are feeling. They do not pay attention. Negative emotions have a way of getting noticed, by showing up as irritation, anger, or depression. How in tune are you with your present emotions? What do you do to generate positive emotions?

In The Classroom

In the classroom, you will deal with students who bring a wide variety of emotions. Many kids will not be able to identify or cope with overwhelming emotions. They will not understand how to regulate and manage them. Many will act without thinking.

An increase in emotional intelligence strengthens our awareness of emotions and makes it possible to be proactive with them. For example, perhaps a child is experiencing fear. How can we help him or her to cope? I talk with the student and together we brainstorm strategies. Recognizing and naming the emotion is the first step.

Sharing potential causes might be the second. Expressing the fear by journaling or discussing it might be the third.

On a Personal Note...

I was fortunate enough to study emotional intelligence during my teacher credential program. I discovered that emotional intelligence is just as important as one's intellectual quotient. If we do not have a grasp of our own emotions, it can be very difficult to help students with their unique needs.

Action for the Day

- ✓ Today, ask yourself how you take care of yourself emotionally. Are you in touch with your emotions? Do you recognize your normal emotional range? If you are aware of what you are feeling, you can expand upon it or change it. Practicing the three steps identified above is a beginning.

6 Seconds Moment

- ◆ Take six seconds to stop and identify with your current emotions.

#180.
Being Naïve

"I was so naive as a kid I used to sneak behind the barn and do nothing."
Johnny Carson

Concept for Today

When have you been naïve? Being naïve is a part of everyone's life path. Experience helps us to avoid the error the next time. Each time that we are naïve, we must remember that life gives us the precious gift of discernment.

In The Classroom

I began my teaching career as a substitute. I was so excited, yet very naïve. I once substituted in a high school for kids on probation. At the end of the period, I looked down at the floor and noticed that there were pink post-it notes all over the carpet. I questioned the kids but no one could explain. As I began picking up the post-its, I then noticed one on my sleeve that said, "Kick me." How did I miss all of these occurrences?

On a Personal Note...

I entered the profession with naïveté. I thought that I knew everything about substitute teaching and classroom management. However, I learned from experience that students will definitely test a new teacher. Now, I have grown those "eyes in the back of my head."

Action for the Day

- ✓ Today, write down something that you have done in your life that was naïve. How do you feel about it now? Would you do anything differently?

6 Seconds Moment

- ◆ Take six seconds to value the times in your life when you were naïve. Honor yourself for making the foolish mistakes in your life, because they have shaped you into the person you are today.

#181.
The Road More Traveled

"There are only two ways to live your life. One is as though nothing is a miracle. The other is as though everything is a miracle."
Albert Einstein

Concept for Today

Do you travel the road "more" traveled which is often filled with simply existing, being negative, hurried and bored, or do you take the road which is filled with optimism? When we first began to walk, talk, and relate to people, we were filled with optimism, joy, and happiness. Somewhere along the road of life, we may have had our hearts broken, experienced failures, deceit, and disappointment. Do we give up and let life's wounds disease our thinking? Or do we practice the steps of optimism and apply a band-aid to life's hurts?

In The Classroom

Teaching our kids to be optimistic is one of the greatest gifts that we can give them. We cannot shelter our kids. We do, however, want them strong and resilient. We want them to be able to bounce back and recover from any situation optimistically and positively.

On a Personal Note…

I have traveled down the road of martyrdom, cynicism, resentment, and self-centeredness. What a lonely and terrifying road. However, due to my unpleasant travels, I have discovered a new road which is filled with optimism, gratitude, joy, and peace. There still may be times in my life when I will take detours off the optimistic road, but I only diverge for a short time.

Action for the Day

- ✓ Today, ask yourself if your optimism shows itself on a daily basis. What do you do when it is challenged? Forge ahead, or get side tracked?

6 Seconds Moment

- ◆ Take six seconds to decide if you will take the road filled with optimism or travel the road filled with pessimism.

#182.
Surprises

"Surprise is the greatest gift which life can grant us."
Boris Pasternak

Concept for Today

Life is filled with surprises, sometimes good and sometimes horrific. Are you the type of person who enjoys surprise parties? Has anyone ever thrown you a surprise party? Do you travel through life expecting unpleasant surprises such as car troubles, unexpected bills, a sudden illness or accident? The difficult surprises build our resiliency.

In The Classroom

There will always be surprises, both good and bad. For example, you may feel exhausted and discouraged after relentlessly teaching a student who still does not grasp the material. You may feel like giving up, but then, out of the blue, the student "surprises" you and finally understands the material. There may be other surprises, such as implementing a brand new lesson which bombs and is not as effective as you had hoped. Also, there will be many times when you will receive a "surprise" visit from your principal. However, there will also be joyous surprises such as thank you cards, smiles, kind words, and charming little presents from your students.

On a Personal Note…

I realize that life never stays the same. There will always be surprises. Fortunately, my heart and mind are receptive and I am grateful for the "nice surprises" which life has to offer. Hopefully, I am emotionally prepared for the "not-so-nice" surprises.

Action for the Day

- ✓ Today, keep your heart open and resiliency up for life's surprises. Make a plan to surprise a good friend with a small gift or card.

6 Seconds Moment

- ◆ Take six seconds to make a decision to embrace and appreciate life's little surprises.

#183. Procrastination

"Procrastination is the thief of time."
Edward Young

Concept for Today

I woke up this morning realizing that I was very tired of hanging on to unresolved problems which had been placed on the back burner. There was the form that I needed to complete, plus a conference to schedule with my daughter's teacher. I needed to make a phone call to manage my student loan re-payment schedule; I needed to research why my rent was going to be increased; and I needed to balance my check book. The list goes on. It appeared that procrastination was showing its ugly face.

I decided to free myself of guilt and piled-up tasks. This was not a one time shot, but a way of life that I needed to adopt permanently. Admitting that I had a problem with procrastination, I decided to start slowly, and work on one task at a time.

In The Classroom

In the classroom, I had also procrastinated with unwanted tasks such as filing, making phone calls, doing my classroom order forms, and organizing my supply closet. I determined to tackle the filing first, by putting away five folders each day at lunchtime.

On a Personal Note…

For myself, there are times when I still procrastinate. A powerful and effective system for accomplishing tasks is to write each one down on a list, cut them out and place in a hat. Pull out one task, and make a conscious decision to accomplish it that day. This ritual will empower you and give you motivation to avoid "pile-ups."

Action for the Day

- ✓ Today, ask yourself if you tend to procrastinate. What does it feel like to have life's irritating tasks pile up on you? What can you do to change the behavior? How do you feel when you accomplish things that make your life easier?

6 Seconds Moment

- ◆ Take six seconds to identify (or brainstorm) several ways to kick the procrastination habit.

#184.
Being Silly

"Mix a little foolishness with your serious plans. It is lovely to be silly at the right moment."
Horace

Concept for Today

Having fun and being silly are wonderful outlets for everyone. We are never too old to giggle. Do you ever catch yourself being silly? Sometimes, when I get overtired, the silliness just spills out.

In The Classroom

One of the nicest compliments that I can ever receive is when students tell me that I am funny. I was the instructor in Juvenile Hall, teaching the students most likely to be sent on to prison. As a reward, I would allow students to listen to the radio. They agreed upon a Classic Soul station which was enjoyed by students and myself. This particular day, when an old hot song came on the radio, I broke out into a full robot dance. The students loved it and "egged me on." I remember the guard, who sat in my room, laughed so hard that he almost fell off the chair. As I danced, I had a few students join me. My classroom turned into "crazy dance party." The only thing we needed was a disco ball and platform shoes. I realized that I had created a deep sense of mutual trust with the students. I knew that I was doing something right because these kids, who were facing prison, were able to laugh and enjoy the moment.

On a Personal Note…

People always told me not to be so serious. After years of being super serious, I have learned to lighten up and laugh.

Action for the Day

✓ Today, think about being silly. Do you ever use silliness in your classroom? If so, give some examples. Do you have a sense of humor? Do you giggle when you are nervous? Is your classroom a place where everyone can laugh?

6 Seconds Moment

◆ Take six seconds to remind yourself that it is okay to be goofy. Make a plan for being silly by noon.

#185.
A Vision For You

"Your vision will become clear only when you look into your heart. Who looks outside, dreams. Who looks inside, awakens."
Carl Jung

Concept for Today

What are your dreams and hopes for your career? How far do you want to go in this occupation? Perhaps you will write a textbook or teach college part time. Maybe you will become a curriculum director or open your own school. Perhaps, you will star in a video highlighting best teacher practices. Maybe you will become a mentor teacher. There are many career opportunities in teaching, just open up your heart and allow yourself to enjoy the experience.

In The Classroom

We must guide students to create their own visions for their futures. Students can paint the most wonderful dreams, visions, hopes, and imaginings. We are the art directors feeding them visions, color schemes, and designs for their canvases.

On a Personal Note...

Today, I have a vision of what the ideal classroom would look like. It is a place that has radiant learning, creative freedom, much needed safety, incredible exploration, and dynamic imagination. It is a place where great learning takes place in a soothing and peaceful environment. I have a vision for what skills and lessons I want my students to have when they leave my classroom. They will be able to: ask questions, work with others, know their learning styles, implement strong study skills, and will have strong conflict resolution skills. They will begin to know who they are as human beings and will be able to rise up and face any challenges with wisdom, humanism, and dignity.

Action for the Day

- ✓ Today, take time to write your vision for your career. Where do you see yourself in ten years? What is your vision for your students and teaching practices? Do you believe that the Teacher's Promise will come true for you? Why or why not?

6 Seconds Moment

- ◆ Take six seconds to make a copy of the Teacher's Promise found at the beginning of this book and then post it in your classroom.

Acknowledgements

I send immense gratitude and true thanksgiving to four of the most brilliant, gifted, creative people who have ever graced the face of earth. Anabel Jensen, Marsha Rideout, Alison Golden, and Caleb Jensen who impact the world with a positive, unique touch of excellence each and every day.

You are leaders among men and women and are truly making a difference 6 seconds at a time. Your wisdom, diligence, time, and patience throughout this book are extraordinary and truly appreciated. Thank you for staying dedicated to our Daily Dose of Optimism Journal.

About The Author

Aline M. Kaprive is an educator with 25 years of teaching experience.

Aline believes that to avoid compassion fatigue in the classroom one must replenish emotionally in order to love unconditionally. When you enter her classroom, there is a sense of well-being, engagement, and enthusiasm. The positive energy is contagious and children learn and achieve academic and emotional goals.

To begin her career, Aline worked as a recreation leader in which she planned and implemented arts and crafts, science, and educational games to a diverse population. She then went on to teach pre-school where she used a wide variety of strategies for the little ones to keep them laughing and engaged. Her true passion blossomed when she began working with incarcerated youth with special needs.

Aline was in her essence when she began teaching the most troubled of students and helping them to discover their educational potential and soar to new heights in a classroom setting. She worked magic by accessing different learning modalities and making education exciting.

Can you imagine incarcerated youth creating different bubble solutions, taking data, and then being on the Juvenile Hall quad measuring the time that each bubble would last before it popped? Or perhaps being given permission to make paper airplanes while writing down directions to be shared with a partner who would make a duplicate airplane and later hold a distance race with their creations?

Aline has three teaching credentials from Notre Dame de Namur University and a Masters Degree in Education She has now taught incarcerated youth for over 10 years. She lives in the San Francisco Bay Area with her husband, daughter and their dog, Trixie.

About the Editors

Anabel L. Jensen, Ph.D., is the President of Six Seconds, the largest organization supporting development in emotional intelligence globally, and a master teacher and pioneer in emotional intelligence education.

A two-time Federal Blue Ribbon winner for excellence in education, she was Executive Director of the Nueva School from 1983 to 1997 where she helped develop the Self-Science curriculum featured in Daniel Goleman's bestselling book, *Emotional Intelligence*.

She is a world-leading expert on how to teach emotional intelligence and a full professor at the Notre Dame De Namur University and Department Chair of the College of Education, NDNU. Her noble goal is to "teach accountability and compassion so that ethical decisions will flood the globe."

After teaching for several years in public school primary grades, **Marsha Rideout** continued her life's work as an administrator, middle school advisor, and Self-Science teacher. In 1997, she joined Dr. Jensen in starting Six Seconds.

Marsha is co-author of *Self-Science: the Emotional Intelligence Curriculum,* as well as the *Handle With Care Emotional Intelligence Activity Book* and several editions of the *Handle With Care Emotional Intelligence Activity Calendar*. She continues to incorporate the latest research and practices into the SEL curriculum and admissions procedures.

Made in the USA
Charleston, SC
16 October 2013